None of These Things Move Me

The Leslie Hale Story

None of These Things Move Me

The Leslie Hale Story

Leslie Hale

Ambassador International
Greenville, South Carolina & Belfast, Northern Ireland
www.ambassador-international.com

None of These Things Move Me

The Leslie Hale Story

© 2009 Leslie Hale

Printed in the United States of America

ISBN 978-1-932307-52-8

Cover Design & Page Layout by David Siglin of A&E Media

Cover photograph by LaDonna Raquel (Hale) Harvey.

Published by
AMBASSADOR INTERNATIONAL
Emerald House
427 Wade Hampton Blvd.
Greenville, SC 29609, USA
www.ambassador-international.com

For
LESLIE HALE MINISTRIES
P. O. Box 125
Tarpon Springs, FL 34688, USA
www.lesliehale.com
leslie@lesliehale.com
(727) 938-0112

DEDICATION

Sometimes I think that I should write to the publishers of Webster's Dictionary. I have a suggestion for them. Instead of writing words of explanation under "Christian" they should just show a photograph of my two sisters—Doreen and Ella. Doreen and Ella are magnificent. All our family here in America love them so very dearly. They are so kind, so loving, so encouraging day after day, month after month, year after year. No man ever had two greater sisters.

Doreen and Ella, thank you a million times over for being— Doreen and Ella! You are both magnificent beyond words!

Your eternally loving brother—Leslie.

TABLE OF CONTENTS

NONE OF THESE THINGS MOVES ME.

-PAUL (ACTS 20:24)

PREFACE

Leslie and Maureen Hale are friends, pastors, role models, confidantes, and two people with a mighty call of God upon their lives...

When I was asked to write the preface of this new exciting book, I got to thinking firstly "exactly how long have I known Leslie and Maureen Hale?" I was shocked when I realized it was over forty-eight years ago when my parents first took me to hear Leslie preach at their church - Faith Tabernacle on York Road in Belfast, Northern Ireland. I would probably have been about seven or eight years of age.

I believe in the "walk of life" that there are special periods when, on looking back, you realize how significant and special they were. Well that was one of those significant times for me. I remember those meetings so well, even at that young age. I can still remember standing in the book shop within the church and saying to my parents, "*when I am older I am going to work for Leslie & Maureen Hale in their church.*" That became my life's ambition. That was in the very early sixties but then, even as a child, I knew God wanted me to be a part of their ministry.

As I grew into my teenage years and adulthood, it was still my ambition to be a part of the Leslie Hale Ministry. I will never forget the day back in the early seventies when Leslie and Maureen took me out to lunch, then back to their house as Leslie said he wanted to discuss something with me. As I sat playing with their youngest daughter, LaDonna, who would have been about seven months old, I was full of anticipation and excitement wondering what exactly they wanted to say.

What joy and excitement filled my soul when Leslie asked me if I would become the church secretary and later the church administrator. I must have said YES a million times, but Leslie insisted that I talk with my parents first. On reflection, I suppose they too knew what the answer would be. They also knew the desire of my heart and God's call on my life, so they gave me their blessing. I can hardly believe that was in December 1974 (wow) thirty-five years ago, can you imagine that?

I suppose after all this time I can truly say that I _KNOW_ Leslie and Maureen Hale; I know their sterling character, their impeccable honesty, and their unblemished morals. As a family they have always been such examples to others. God was and is the head of their house and that is what makes it such a successful, happy one.

In those thirty-five years, what experiences I have witnessed and gained, what miracles I have seen in that time. I have seen literally thousands upon thousands of people accept Jesus as their Saviour, countless people healed by Gods power, and many people delivered from demon possession.

I remember the first time I witnessed a young girl be completely set free from demon forces ... what a night that was! It took several strong men to hold that young, slim, girl down. To hear the deep voice emerge from her was incredible. I remember Leslie standing back and saying these amazing words, "DEVIL, WHAT HAPPENED AT CALVARY?" That young woman screamed, twisted, and yelled – but she could not answer. God showed Leslie exactly how many demons possessed that young girl, and he prayed and cast them out.

A blood-curdling cry came from that young girl; she was about fifteen years of age and _immediately_ those demons vacated her body. A peace and calm came over her body and in her normal voice, she cried out to God and surrendered her life to Him. I knew that young girl very well, still do, and am happy to say that she and her husband are still serving the Lord to this very day. That must have happened in the early seventies. I can remember scenes like this being repeated time and time again.

When I think of the miracles I have seen, I thank God that Leslie and Maureen went through with Him and His obvious call on their lives, despite going through many battles.

I guess it is hard to calculate how many people accepted Christ as their Saviour. Many of those people are now on the mission field or are pastors or ministers with their own thriving churches. Many have gone on to meet the Redeemer he introduced them to, after serving Him for many years.

All this would never have been possible without the relentless obedience of Leslie and Maureen to the call of God and the untold sacrifices they made throughout the years.

Leslie Hale is a man "sold out" to God and His Word. The impact on people's lives that his preaching has made is amazing. On meeting people who attended the services in Faith Tabernacle and Faith Cathedral, they are of one voice .... *"No one could expound on God's Word like him"*. One person I met within the past week reminded me of a message Leslie preached in the early seventies called "Freedom from Fear" and how after listening to that message, God set her free from a gripping fear she had been dealing with for over eight years and to this day is still free! Leslie Hale preached the uncompromised Word of God which resulted in untold numbers of lives being changed.

The sad thing was jealous men tried to stop his voice and threatened to take over his ministry; in fact, one man tried to *steal* it. Remember, I was the church secretary. I was on the "inside" of what was happening, what I am stating here is 100% factual.

Not to dwell on the negative, but there were those who got so jealous of his ministry that they deliberately set out to try to destroy it by lying about him. I remember the day the police arrived. A person had gone to the police. Of course, the whole thing was 100% absurd but the press had a field day with that one. One thing I do recall was that during this time, there was an overwhelming peace and calm in my heart. I guess this is what the Bible means when it says, "a peace that passeth all understanding." Upon investigation the authorities wrote to us with the words, *NO CASE TO ANSWER!!!!!* Praise the Lord. (Not surprisingly, the press were not interested in that one!) It was so sad to hear the lies that had been told about the ministry and the persecution that Leslie and Maureen both went through, but on looking back, as the scriptures said, "God delivered us out of them *ALL.*"

I remember one time we were trying to get planning permission for the new church building. Oh, how those people in the planning office hated us. I recall having an appointment in their office, when the guy behind the desk said (in some words I cannot repeat!) that "we would NEVER, never get planning permission for our new church." Thank God, our Lord knew otherwise!!!!!

I will always be eternally grateful that Leslie and Maureen went through with God, despite these battles and trials. At times it must have been so hard for them, with the press constantly hounding them, writing lies, etc. If they couldn't get a story, they simply made one up.

I remember a well-known journalist ended a program he was presenting about Leslie and his ministry here in Ireland. In his summary he said an amazing line, "*I believe that this man has been sinned against rather than sinned.*" How true this was.

Personally I feel that because of these trials, I am a much better person today. I have learned that despite the circumstances, GOD HAS EVERYTHING UNDER HIS CONTROL. I have learned to TOTALLY lean on Him at ALL TIMES.

Leslie knows God's voice. When God suddenly called him from Ireland to America, Leslie immediately obeyed. He would also have obeyed if God had called him to Africa. I can clearly see God's hand in it. America has given Leslie a freedom to preach God's Word that he did not have in Ireland.

As you read this book, I trust that you will see the Leslie and Maureen Hale who I know and love—two people who have sacrificed so many things to fulfil the call of God on their lives. People who live by example, who put God first, who love God, and who preach the uncompromised Word of God. I, like untold multitudes, thank God for them. I have known them for over forty years. I have never met a more honourable, honest, and moral couple. The most striking thing about them is their obedience to God. Whether it is Ireland or America or Africa or anywhere else, you can be sure that they are going to obey the Lord Jesus whom they love with all their hearts. You will be a much richer person by getting to know and listen to Leslie and Maureen Hale.

Joan Lonsdale
Belfast, Northern Ireland

FOREWORD

My name is Ella Hale. I am Leslie's sister. At the time of writing I am eighty years of age. In some ways, at least in part, I am responsible for the writing of this book. For many years I have urged my brother Leslie to put down "in black and white" the details of what has happened in his ministry. Even though I started my "urgings" many years ago, it is only recently that Leslie has decided to record so many of the phenomenal things which have happened to him, both in his personal life and in his public ministry. I, along with Leslie and our sister Doreen, were raised by our fantastic parents to always tell the truth. What you will read in this book is the truth about Leslie Hale.

Obviously, I am in a position to know. I am several years older than Leslie. I remember the time he was born and how he was raised as a little boy in our home. It was abundantly clear from early on that God's almighty hand was upon Leslie. He was a wonderful child and both of our parents were so proud of him, right up until they passed away.

Leslie has a fierce commitment to the will of God. He has let nothing stop him from doing what God has told him to do. I have watched him walk with God for well over fifty years. Not just in the pulpit, but behind closed doors. To say the least, he is a mighty chosen vessel of the King of Kings and Lord of Lords. Actually, he never ceases to amaze me. He is so quiet and unassuming even to the point of shyness, that is, until he gets into the pulpit then he becomes like a tiger or a tornado. His skill in preaching and teaching God's Word is simply breath-taking. He digs and digs into the Scriptures and then has a tremendous gift in communicating those glorious truths to his listeners. People listen to him, of course, all over the world. He is loving and kind and mannerly. He is, to Doreen and I, the greatest brother in the whole world, and the greatest brother we could ever have wished for. For the last number of years, Doreen and I have visited with Leslie and Maureen for four or five months each year. We stay in their home and enjoy the beautiful Florida sunshine.

Perhaps the most striking thing about Leslie is the anointing which rests upon his life. He is so fervently in love with God and God's presence fills his very being. It's not very often in life that you meet a person who is so close to God. Leslie could say for sure, "for He walks with me and He talks with me and He tells me I am His own."

The strange thing is that he never wanted to be a preacher. To this day he has no love for the pulpit. His love and obedience is to God and if that includes preaching and teaching, so be it. However, his desire is not to preach but rather to love and obey Jesus. I can honestly say Leslie loves Jesus with every fiber of his being. Jesus and Leslie are best friends. You see I have witnessed it "up-close" for well over fifty years. His work and ministry are based in Florida. From there he reaches out around the world. A visit to his headquarters is awe-inspiring. The services in the magnificent sanctuary, the fabulous dining facility, and the tremendous Antique Bible Museum are all so dynamic. There is no doubt that God wanted all this for Glengormley in Northern Ireland but when the day came that God led Leslie away from Ireland, he could do nothing but obey God and "shake the dust from off his feet." (Matthew 10:14) What a loss for Northern Ireland!

On one occasion when Pastor and Mrs. George Brown (who had been our pastors for a period in Belfast where our family attended the Church of the Nazarene) were in Florida and heard Leslie speak, they were both overcome. Pastor George declared, "That was the greatest message I ever heard in my entire life." Mrs. Brown added something very significant. "What a loss," she said. "What a loss for Northern Ireland!" God, I suppose, must have got tired of those evil people who constantly lied about Leslie and tried to destroy his ministry in Ireland that He finally instructed Leslie to leave and, as I say, he was to "shake the dust from off his feet." Leslie, you will see, will tell more about all that in the following pages.

Finally let me say the following things with great clarity and emphasis.

(1) My brother Leslie is a servant of God who has consistently obeyed God and walked with Him in spite of all opposition and lies told against him. Remember, as an eighty year old, I am telling you the whole truth.

(2) I can clearly recall many years ago when one particular person rose up against Leslie to try to destroy him. In some ways it is a pity that I have to mention him at all since there are so many wonderful things to talk about regarding Leslie's life and calling. However, it is part of the story so let me mention it briefly. It so happens that I know the person who fought Leslie so viciously. I know him extremely well. **I also know the facts.** I have never, in my 80 years seen a man so filled with jealousy, lies, and hatred as that person. He was consumed with the idea of destroying Leslie. The Bible says, "They hated me without a cause." (John 15:25) Not only did that person have no cause - it was the exact opposite. Leslie had been so good to that person. He gave him money. He sustained his family. Leslie knew the facts about that man, how he had been in trouble with his employer, and how he had had an affair with the wife of one of the men in Faith Tabernacle. Yet, as that man stormed around trying to destroy Leslie, Leslie, in turn, did not tell the facts about that man to others.

Not only did that man seek to destroy Leslie, when he found he could not do that, he tormented my sister Doreeen and myself and our parents in spite of their advancing years. Oh how ugly are the powers of darkness!

It so happens that I knew that man's parents exceptionally well also. Very, very well. His own mother said to me, "Satan has entered into him." His own father said in my hearing, "Don't ever let anybody ever know that that fellow was ever my son - and don't let him attend my funeral!"

Yet Leslie stayed calm through it all. In fact, at that very time, the Holy Spirit gave Leslie these powerful words, "The people who matter are for you." That evil, lying man has been miserable, but Leslie has blazed ahead living for God and obeying His commands. You should listen to Leslie Hale. I tell you that not just because he is my brother, but because he is in touch with God and will bless you mightily as he ministers God's Word to you.

When we look back 2,000 years ago it seems unbelievable that so much hatred could have been poured out against Jesus. Jesus was so good and loving and kind, yet people, filled with Satan, wanted Him destroyed. It has been that way with the servants of God also. It is still that way today. "Yea, and all that will live godly in Christ Jesus shall suffer persecution." (2 Timothy 3:12) However, God has an amazing way of bringing good out of bad. God does not send the bad, but He brings good out of it. They killed Jesus and thus He became the Saviour of the world. Joseph said, "But as for you, ye thought evil against me; but God meant it unto good, to bring to pass, as it is this day, to save much people alive." (Genesis 50:20)

Paul said, "I will turn to the gentiles" (Acts 13:46) and so we got the gospel. When Leslie, at God's clear instructions, left Ireland and launched his vision in America, it was a world of difference. What a thrill it is to see a big-minded person working with big-minded people. As well as the thrill of ministry in America, Leslie's whole family love living in America. They are all so much in the center of God's will! God gets the last laugh. As you read the following pages, you will see the glorious way God has blessed Leslie and his ministry. It is all a result of obeying God. What is also incredible is the way God's original vision given to Leslie is being fulfilled exactly as God stated. However, it is in Florida and not in Northern Ireland.

My sister Doreen, who is a little older than I, wanted it to be made clear that she "seconds" and agrees with every word recorded in this foreword.

In closing, I would like to say a little word about our parents, Dorcas and "Scottie" Hale. Leslie, Doreen, and I are so proud of them. They raised us right. Our mother used to sing a little song, "It's a sin to tell a lie." That was the way we were raised in our happy home. Our Daddy, "Scottie" Hale, was a famous accordionist. After retiring, he became the printer for Leslie's ministry. In fact, he passed away in Leslie's arms. Doreen, Leslie, and I honored both our parents so much. I wish I could end by saying that everything was perfect for them until they passed away. However, that is not so. They were hurt and tormented from a certain source without let-up until their passing. It should be noted that Doreen, Leslie, and I honored them and that is why God has honored us.

Leslie has come through his battles gloriously. If the man in Belfast who tried to destroy him had had anything of substance against Leslie, that man would have told the world. He had nothing but hatred and lies, and his lies soon collapsed under their own weight. That man could have been filled with the Holy Ghost. Instead of that, he was and is sadly in the grip of despair.

WHO WOULD TRUE VALOUR SEE

Who would true Valour see
Let him come hither;
One here will Constant be,
Come Wind, come Weather.
There's no Discouragement,
Shall make him once Relent,
His first avow'd Intent,
  To be a Pilgrim.

Who so beset him round,
With dismal stories,
Do but themselves confound;
His Strength the more is.
No Lion can him fright,
He'll with a Giant fight,
But he will have a right,
  To be a Pilgrim.

Hobgoblin, nor foul Fiend,
Can daunt his Spirit:
He knows, he at the end,
Shall Life Inherit.
Then Fancies fly away,
He'll fear not what men say,
He'll labour Night and Day,
  To be a Pilgrim.

John Bunyan

CHAPTER I

CONFRONTATION

I was sitting in the parking lot of Carrickfergus Castle in Carrickfergus, County Antrim, Northern Ireland. Carrick is about ten miles from Belfast. The great castle, jutting out into the water, was sitting there 650 years before America became a nation.

Sitting in the car with me was a man I had loved fervently. I had done everything I could to help him. This incident happened many years ago. I was still a young preacher but I knew two things for sure - I loved God with all my heart, and I was living in obedience to Him. He had called me to preach, and I was carrying out His will in my life.

This man sitting beside me was a tormented soul. He had told me several times that he knew he was the re-incarnation of Judas Iscariot. He seemed to be a rational person, but there was a horrific darkness upon him. I had remembered some years before when we were playing soccer how he had run at great speed straight into a brick wall and hit his head. I wondered if that had left its mark. Anyway, he couldn't shake the "absolute certainty" he said he had regarding Judas Iscariot. He had gotten into some kind of trouble at the place of his employment, and I had sustained him and his family for quite a period, financially. This did not count the money he took from my ministry behind my back and without my permission, which I found out about later. Now, I am sitting in the car. I am called of God and God's power was in my being. He, on the other hand, was totally miserable.

On another occasion, I brought him to my home to seek to pray this thing through. I really wanted him to find deliverance. I asked him to join me kneeling at the side of the bed. We did. I said that we would both pray, but that he should pray first. Silence.

Not a word. He then said that he could not pray. I said, "All right, I'll pray and you repeat the prayer after me." I determined to keep the prayer short and simple. I started by saying "Jesus." Again there was silence. I repeated, "Say Jesus." He then blurted out these amazing words. "I can't," he said, "because that name (Jesus) sticks in my throat."

To say that I had a difficult case on my hands puts it mildly. On yet another occasion, I found out he was lying about me to some of the men of the church. He was totally caught off guard when I called a snap meeting of the congregation. It was a Thursday night and several people came. I always remember Cyril Morton, one of the men of the church. He had just heard about the meeting and said to me just before it started, "Leslie, I don't know what this is about, but I just want you to know that I am for you all the way." How I loved Cyril and his family. Such loyalty! It was so refreshing. The meeting started and I brought up this man's lies. I wanted to know if anybody had anything to say. He sat as if frozen to the seat. A few of the people he had gossiped to said a few things which amounted to nothing at all. I had a sheaf of papers with me and after I had asked if anybody else had anything to say —and they had not—I then said that I had a few things to say, and I would read them from my papers. At that second the trouble-maker jumped to his feet and with a trembling voice asked if he could talk things over with me privately. I smiled inside. I brought the meeting to a close without ever reading what was written on my papers. I knew what was there and so did he. It was details of an affair he had with the wife of one of the men who was sitting in that meeting! Wow!

Now, back to the parking lot in Carrickfergus. We were sitting in the car. I was still trying to help him. I was absolutely getting nowhere. Then, an unbelievable thing happened. He turned and looked at me. We were both sitting in the front seats of a small car so our faces were pretty close to each other. He then stared at me and in a totally ice-cold way, said these words, "My mission in life is to destroy your mission in life." I wept. Not because I was afraid of him or anything he would try to do to me, but it was obvious he was totally in Satan's hands. I had done everything, financially and otherwise, to help him and his wife and children, but it was all to no avail. He was a prisoner of Satan and that was obvious.

Over the next decades that man stayed true to "his mission." I never did a thing to him or his family other than good. The Bible says, "They hated me without a cause." (John 15:25) He was filled with anger, jealousy, and envy, and he was going to take it out on me. I would like to ask my reader, "Have you ever had anything like that said or done to you?" This man went out and lied about me everywhere. Even his own mother said, "Satan has entered into him." He became a total tool of Satan, dedicated, through outright lies and slander, to destroy my life and ministry. In fact both of us stayed true to our mission. I have stayed true to God in obeying Him and taking His Gospel all over the world. That other man stayed true to his mission in seeking to destroy me.

To this day, I am still blessed and to this day, he is still miserable. It is obvious that if this wretched man had had something on me, he would have told the whole world about it. He had nothing, so he has had to use innuendo, slander, gossip, and lies. He has been consistent year after year, decade after decade; all without cause or foundation. Over the years, I have not concentrated upon this man at all. In fact, I couldn't care less. Of course, it comes back to me now that I am writing this story. It's hard to believe what happened and what was said to me that day in the parking lot of Carrickfergus Castle. A few days before the snap meeting which I called, the Lord "lit up" two Psalms for me. Here they are:

PSALM 35
Plead my cause, O LORD, with them that strive with me: fight against them that fight against me.
Take hold of shield and buckler, and stand up for mine help.
Draw out also the spear, and stop the way against them that persecute me: say unto my soul, I am thy salvation.
Let them be confounded and put to shame that seek after my soul: let them be turned back and brought to confusion that devise my hurt.
Let them be as chaff before the wind: and let the angel of the LORD chase them.
Let their way be dark and slippery: and let the angel of the LORD persecute them.

For without cause have they hid for me their net in a pit, which without cause they have digged for my soul.

Let destruction come upon him at unawares; and let his net that he hath hid catch himself: into that very destruction let him fall.

And my soul shall be joyful in the LORD: it shall rejoice in His salvation.

All my bones shall say, LORD, who is like unto thee, which deliverest the poor from him that is too strong for him, yea, the poor and the needy from him that spoileth him?

False witnesses did rise up; they laid to my charge things that I knew not.

They rewarded me evil for good to the spoiling of my soul.

But as for me, when they were sick, my clothing was sackcloth: I humbled my soul with fasting; and my prayer returned into mine own bosom.

I behaved myself as though he had been my friend or brother: I bowed down heavily, as one that mourneth for his mother.

But in mine adversity they rejoiced, and gathered themselves together: yea, the abjects gathered themselves together against me, and I knew it not; they did tear me, and ceased not:

With hypocritical mockers in feasts, they gnashed upon me with their teeth.

Lord, how long wilt thou look on? rescue my soul from their destructions, my darling from the lions.

I will give thee thanks in the great congregation: I will praise thee among much people.

Let not them that are mine enemies wrongfully rejoice over me: neither let them wink with the eye that hate me without a cause.

For they speak not peace: but they devise deceitful matters against them that are quiet in the land.

Yea, they opened their mouth wide against me, and said, Aha, aha, our eye hath seen it.

This thou hast seen, O LORD: keep not silence: O Lord, be not far from me.

Stir up thyself, and awake to my judgment, even unto my cause, my God and my Lord.

Judge me, O LORD my God, according to thy righteousness; and let them not rejoice over me.

Let them not say in their hearts, Ah, so would we have it: let them not say, We have swallowed him up.

Let them be ashamed and brought to confusion together that rejoice at mine hurt: let them be clothed with shame and dishonour that magnify themselves against me.

Let them shout for joy, and be glad, that favour my righteous cause: yea, let them say continually, Let the LORD be magnified, which hath pleasure in the prosperity of his servant.

And my tongue shall speak of thy righteousness and of thy praise all the day long.

PSALM 57
Be merciful unto me, O God, be merciful unto me: for my soul trusteth in thee: yea, in the shadow of thy wings will I make my refuge, until these calamities be overpast.

I will cry unto God most high; unto God that performeth all things for me.

He shall send from heaven, and save me from the reproach of Him that would swallow me up. Selah. God shall send forth His mercy and His truth.

My soul is among lions: and I lie even among them that are set on fire, even the sons of men, whose teeth are spears and arrows, and their tongue a sharp sword.

Be thou exalted, O God, above the heavens; let thy glory be above all the earth.

They have prepared a net for my steps; my soul is bowed down: they have digged a pit before me, into the midst whereof they are fallen themselves. Selah.

My heart is fixed, O God, my heart is fixed: I will sing and give praise.

Awake up, my glory; awake, psaltery and harp: I myself will awake early.

I will praise thee, O Lord, among the people: I will sing unto thee among the nations.

For thy mercy is great unto the heavens, and thy truth unto the clouds.

Be thou exalted, O God, above the heavens: let thy glory be above all the earth.

On the evening of the "meeting of confrontation," I was standing in my living room talking to my wife, Maureen and a friend. We were about to leave for the meeting. Suddenly, the Holy Spirit rose up in me and instructed me to go to my bedroom alone. There He spoke to me clearly. "You will return from this meeting tonight victoriously!!" We did!! All I can say is "Hallelujah!!"

PSALM 62

My soul with expectation doth
Depend on God indeed:
My strength and my salvation do
From him alone proceed.

He only my salvation is,
And my strong rock is he:
He only is my sure defence;
Much moved I shall not be.

Only on God do thou, my soul,
Still patiently attend;
My expectation and my hope
On him alone depend.

He only my salvation is,
And my strong rock is he;
He only is my sure defence:
I shall not moved be.

In God my glory placed is,
And my salvation sure;
In God the rock is of my strength,
My refuge most secure.

Scottish Psalter, 1880

CHAPTER 2

MY WONDERFUL CALLING

I was born at sixteen St. Vincent Street off the Shore Road in Belfast, Northern Ireland. I was the youngest of our family. My father was born in Scotland, in a place called Alexandria beside Balloch, where the waters of Loch Lomond (probably the most famous of all of Scotland's beautiful lochs) come rolling in. My mother was born and raised in Poyntzpass, a tiny village tucked away in County Armagh, Northern Ireland.

I had a very happy childhood, but there were many questions and a good deal of confusion about things in life as I was growing up. Most young people, I suppose, are faced with such questions. This I did know, however; I was possessed of an extremely tender conscience and, as a result, I suffered many battles as I passed through my early teens.

My childhood presented no problems. My father was a tireless worker, always punctual at his place of labour. He provided for the entire family magnificently, and I never knew what it was to have to worry about such things as the provision of our domestic supplies. Who bought the food, the clothes, the furniture? These questions never really came up in my mind. In fact, I suppose that subconsciously, I imagined my father had an unending supply of money. Now that I am older, I realize that was far from the truth. It was just his non-stop working and excellent budgeting that supplied our needs.

My mother was also a tireless worker, always caring for her husband and family. Her dedication to her family was a model of love and service. She was the epitome of motherhood. When we, her family, were hurt, she hurt for us. When her family was joyful, then she shared that joy with us.

My daddy was able to supplement his wages by playing his accordion and by teaching aspiring accordionists. He had his own small orchestra in those days and overcame great difficulties as he tenaciously taught himself music. My father's father was only twenty-eight years old when he died, resulting in a period of great anguish and sorrow for my father.

When I was just a little fellow I would sit on the floor in our house, playing with a few toys and watching daddy playing and practicing the accordion. To put it mildly, he was a genius with that box. The older I have become the greater has become my appreciation for my father. I rate him among the greatest musicians I have ever heard. Many others who had listened to him play, agree. He was almost like a magician with those big fingers and hands! He used to play the first couple of tunes (including "The Flight of the Bumblebee") with a glove on his right hand. Everything would come to a halt and all the people would gather round to watch this remarkable exhibition of musical talent.

My father had his accordions specially manufactured in Italy, and the keys made of mother-of-pearl with his name in reflectors down the front. His instrument was several keys larger than a regular accordion.

It was absolutely breath-taking to watch and listen to him playing "The Light Cavalry Overture" and many other famous pieces.

My father influenced my life greatly. He was always good and kind. He never drank. Once as a child, I was with him and the rest of our family in the home of one of our relations. Somebody brought some alcoholic drink in. I had never seen it in our house and I didn't like the look of it. I felt strange in the atmosphere it had created. My father played some tunes for the guests and everyone was laughing and talking. I was doing neither. I was watching the glass of beer, which someone had poured and set beside my father. As soon as he finished a tune, someone would say, "Scotty, that's for you," pointing to the glass. My eyes never left that glass and my daddy refused the drink each time. When eventually the party was over and we were leaving to go home, that glass was sitting there, still full and untouched. I was so happy and proud. I knew my father didn't drink, but that incident left a tremendous impression upon me. I felt as if I was ten feet tall as I headed for home that night.

My grandfather did not drink either, but after his death my daddy was thrown into situations as a young boy, through which he saw the curse and the sorrows of alcohol. He said that he would never touch alcohol and he never did. He had a great capacity to say "NO!" He used to say to me, "Son, lead. Never be led." He was urging me not to allow myself to be led into foolishness. "You do the leading," he would say. How many people are in terrible trouble today just because they are so easily led? I learned, through my father, to take the initiative in life. He taught me to do something constructive rather than to be led by some foolish person or motive. It has been said that any old dead fish can drift down-stream, but it takes a living one to go up-steam. That still applies today.

I fell in love with soccer when I was a child. I cannot remember when I did not have a soccer ball. I was always playing. This was probably because of two things. St. Vincent Street, where I was born and raised, is right next door to a well-known Northern Ireland Soccer Club, "Crusaders." In fact, I was their ball-boy for a number of years. Later I played on that ground more than once. Between our house and the door into Crusaders' ground was an area called "the field." It actually was an open space strewn with cinders. There I played for hours and hours. I used to head a ball against a wall and then, as it returned, head it again and again against the wall, never letting it touch the ground and never touching it with my hands. I could keep it up hundreds of times. I usually quit only because I was tired or my hair got in my eyes!

The other reason I imagine that I fell in love with soccer was because of enthralling stories my daddy would tell me of great games he had seen as a lad in his native Scotland.

I remember playing at Windsor Park, where Northern Ireland's international games are played. I tried to pick out my father in the crowd but from the pitch, you only see a mass of humanity. In fact, I was already playing at these grounds when I was only a schoolboy. I first saw my name in print in an English newspaper when I was about eleven years old. I had been chosen to play in a representative game. I still remember the game well. We were introduced to a certain dignitary before the game started, and he presented each of us with a ball-point pen! That was something special in those days. That particular match ended in a scoreless draw, but I could count on my fingers the number of times I ended up on the losing side. I played in excellent teams both at Seaview Public Elementary School and later at the Belfast Technical College. In fact, some of Ireland's international stars started their careers on our team.

In fact, a great crisis developed in my life over soccer. When God started dealing with me and calling me to serve Him, it was so serious that I had a clear choice open to me. I either played soccer or served God. There may be some who feel that they can do both. I shall not criticize them whatsoever, but it was not that way with me. It was one or the other. I knew I couldn't do both.

I was saved on my eleventh birthday. That means that every time the 25th of May comes around I have two birthdays, my natural anniversary and my spiritual.

Once when I was on my way home from school, a few days before I accepted Christ, one of my school pals suddenly asked, quite out of the blue, "Leslie aren't you a Christian?" I didn't see anything wrong with being a Christian. In fact deep down I wanted to be one, but I answered honestly, "No Jim, I am not. Why?"

"Well," he said, "You don't swear, you don't go to the pictures (movies), you go to church," and on he went. It is remarkable what goes on inside the minds of little children. I admitted all that he said was true, but emphasized that none of these made me a Christian. Our little talk did, however, make me think more about it.

A few days later, on my eleventh birthday, I signed the pledge of "The Golden Star Brigade" which was a children's outreach of the Christian Herald newspaper. Signing a pledge to "Look Up and Aim High" in itself does not save the soul. However, as I was signing on the line, I also called upon God to save me and for Jesus to come into my heart. I was born again at that second!

Naturally, I did not know much about Theology. I did not know much about anything other than that there was a God and that I needed to be saved; that I had in fact been saved as Jesus came into my heart. I knew these things for sure but beyond them, like most other children, I was in ignorance. A few years later however, things became much more serious. I had just left the Technical High School and was now working in a lawyer's office. I was almost sixteen. I was still very young, but now I had soccer on my mind morning, noon, and night. Just before leaving school, I had been approached by the head sports master who wanted a private talk with me. He told me that I was being chosen, as the only boy out of the entire school, to go and join Northern Ireland's leading soccer club, Linfield. "You will be famous," he told me, "and you'll never need to worry about money for the rest of your life." He said that he had utter confidence in me and in my ability. Then he shook hands with me and wished me well. I said that I would let him know of my decision. Before I had a chance to speak to him again, I left the school and became part of the lawyer's office. His offer still stood. All I had to do was go back to him, tell him of my acceptance, and he would then arrange everything. God, by now, was also dealing with me mightily, calling me to a full dedication to Him. I had been saved when I was eleven years old. Now, however, I was being challenged by God to dedicate myself to Him entirely and to follow His directions for my life.

So there I was in the middle. Some men may feel they can play both football and serve God, but it was clear to me and becoming clearer every day that I would have to choose between them. I could not accommodate both. It was becoming as clear as the mid-day sun to me. It was either God or soccer. Each was too demanding to allow any time for the other. God strove mightily with my soul. How marvelous are the dealings of God with a human being! Nobody, I suppose, looking at me could have known the battle that was going on inside me. The battle was not evident, but to me it was as real as Gettysburg or Waterloo.

What would have happened had I chosen soccer? That must remain forever unanswered. I certainly would not have been happy with myself since I would always have been aware that I had disobeyed God. The very idea of disobeying God is unthinkable to me.

As a soccer player, only time would have told if my sports master's opinion was true or false. Deep within me I believe if I had played soccer I would have made the grade. In fact, I have no doubt whatsoever about it. That may sound very pretentious, but it only serves to underline the fact that I had a very real decision to make.

This feeling of "Certainty" about things has played quite a part in my life. There have been times when I have felt so afraid, so nervous, and so inferior. In fact, a feeling of inferiority has plagued me so many times. At other times, the feeling of certainty utterly grips me and I KNOW that what I am doing is right and that it is going to work. I see and feel that so much in my ministry today.

As I look back, even as a young boy on the soccer field, I can see the same spirit or attitude at work. The other boys used to tease me about how quiet I was as we traveled to a soccer game in the team bus. I was very quiet, but I was also assured. At that time, of course, I did not stop to analyze that assurance, though I was conscious of it. I just knew that we would win. I usually had no doubt that I would score. I never told others of this feeling of KNOWING or CERTAINTY. I never boasted flippantly about us winning. I was very quiet about it all, but inside me I just knew. I was usually the leading goal-scorer, even though I generally played at left-half. I cannot explain this KNOWING, this ASSURANCE, but it has played and is playing a big part in my life. It is such a marvelous feeling to have when things go wrong or when plans seem to be frustrated or delayed. This assurance always brings me through and helps me to keep calm.

Recently, a television reporter asked me about this. We had not been talking about this topic at all, but he had detected it within me. I told him that I could not explain it fully, though I agreed it was there. Do not think that things just sail along perfectly because of this unusual power deep inside me. It may sound extremely paradoxical or even totally contradictory, but I admit I have had times where I have been plagued with a feeling of inferiority. I never wanted to preach. Many times I feel that what I have preached is so simple and obvious that I have insulted the congregation. Sometimes, I am also very shy in meeting people and, to be honest, have avoided it on more than one occasion. I also have a very tender conscience before God and I get extremely upset if I ever feel that I have let Him down.

I have my battles, my hurts, and my troubles. At the bottom of them all, however, there is this practically indefinable assurance. I know what I am doing is right. I know - OH I KNOW - that if I continue to walk humbly before God, He will fulfill His plans for my life and bless multitudes through the exciting ministry which He has given me.

I made my decision on the January 31, 1955. I was supposed to go to night school that evening, but I mentioned to my mother that I was planning to go to a church service instead. After the meeting (there were only a few people there), I went into a side room and knelt down by a bench. I prayed a brief prayer. I told God that I was saying "Yes" to Him, an eternal "Yes." I completely dedicated everything to God that evening. Everything that I had, or would ever have, or even hoped to have was dedicated to Him. All these years later, that dedication still stands. I have never as much as taken the nail of my little finger off the altar of God since that time. I am His totally and I love Him with all my heart. I have never been involved in soccer since that hour. For one thing, I am much too busy. Another reason is simply that when I turned my back on it, I did it for keeps.

Once in a while my wife, Maureen, and I talk about what might have been had I chosen soccer instead of obeying God. I have no regrets whatsoever. However, my life is now taken up with the things of God. It is a much more exciting life and you don't have to retire! In fact, this life lasts for time and eternity.

God's call is powerfully on my life. I have never been to a Bible school or university, but I know that I am called and anointed by God to do what I am doing.

My mother, whose name was Dorcas, knew that I was called before I did. My middle name is Samuel and serves as a reminder of my wonderful calling.

When I was very young I remember my mother pulling me to her side, ruffling my hair with her hand and saying to me, "One day you will be a minister and preach the Gospel." Now I never liked to hurt my mother. I believe in honoring my parents, not in hurting them, so it was very difficult for me to tell her exactly how I felt, that I never wanted to be a preacher! Never! I really don't know why that was unless the image of a minister in my young mind was a bit daunting. He was always dressed in black. He always had to be nice to people. He always had to smile at people and be "nice and proper." Above all, he was always either a sissy or the next thing to one. That was my impression of a minister and perhaps that is why I recoiled in horror when my mother spoke to me of becoming one myself. I didn't tell her what I was thinking, but I certainly wasn't going to preach! That was for sure!

As I have grown into manhood, my impression of ministers has changed somewhat but not entirely. Many still give the impression of being fragile. Many still do dress in black. They rely more on "being nice" to gain friends and members than they do on the power of God. Many of them seem unreal to me. They seem to be removed from the rough and tumble of this world. They seem tailor-made to open ladies' garden fetes and make nice little speeches where they never say anything worthwhile. They seem to have no drive whatsoever.

I know many others who are tremendous, dynamic men. They are real and strong and victorious. They are blessing humanity. I respect these preachers very much. The others leave me cold.

I must emphasize that my mother was not forever telling me that I would be a preacher. She spoke of these things very rarely, but when she did so, I remember the occasions quite clearly. One day, when I was a bit older, she told me how God had spoken at one time to her and given her three verses out of the Bible. As God gave them to her, He said, "These are for your youngest child." This experience reinforced her conviction that God's hand was upon me.

The verses are from Deuteronomy 32:10-12.

"He found him in a desert land, and in the waste howling wilderness; He led him about, He instructed him, He kept him as the apple of His eye. As an eagle stirreth up her nest, fluttereth over her young, spreadeth abroad her wings, taketh them, beareth them on her wings: So the LORD alone did lead him, and there was no strange god with him." My mother used to say to me, "Watchman, what of the night?" (Isaiah 21:11) She also said, "Son, be a watchman on the wall and warn the people."

My mother knew long ago what I was to know with such conviction at a later date. As I look back, I can see how God's hand was upon me from my earliest days of recollection. I must have been a mere seven or eight years old when I would lie on my bed, tears streaming down my cheeks, singing:

"Take my life and let it be,
Consecrated Lord to Thee,
Take my moments and my days,
Let them flow in ceaseless praise."

Another song which moved me deeply as a young boy was one my sister Ella played on the piano.

"If I can help somebody as I pass along,
If I can cheer somebody with a word or song,
If I can show somebody he is traveling wrong,
Then my living shall not be in vain,

Then my living shall not be in vain,
Then my living shall not be in vain,
If I can help somebody as I pass along,
Then my living shall not be in vain."

People have wondered how I was raised politically and what my political opinions are today.

My parents never belonged to a political party, though they always voted at each election. In Northern Ireland, where religion and politics are so closely tied together, I am happy to say that I was never raised to have hatred toward anyone. That is very much a part of my ministry today. In no way am I, nor have I ever been, involved, even remotely, in politics. I realize, of course, that we must have politicians, but it is not my life or calling.

I am bound to express sadness at the behaviour of so many of the politicians during the terrible troubles which dominated Northern Ireland for many years. On too many occasions, the uppermost thoughts seem to have been to score points over each other instead of trying to get together to do something for the good of all the country. One can only speculate what might have happened had the ordinary people not been "fired-up" by the volatile language of so many of their leaders. I am certain that many politicians contributed to the "troubles" by their unrestrained outbursts. I am reminded of the famous words of the American humorist, Mark Twain. "Politicians are the men we have for solving problems which would not be if we had no politicians." That may be taking it a bit far, but leaders, particularly in a situation where lives are at stake, need to think twice and only speak once. I have always been an observer of the political scene, particularly on an international basis. I have some strong views on some issues and on others I am fairly undecided.

I feel however, that as far as I am concerned, they should remain personal views. I do not believe that the pulpit is the place for political speeches. I have read and re-read the words of Jesus in the four Gospels and even though a foreign army was occupying His country, He steered clear of political argument. The reason was, of course, He had something bigger to be involved in.

My ministry is PEOPLE, not for political beliefs or ideas or for folk who follow a certain line of philosophy. If I were involved in politics, I would reduce my calling and my effectiveness for God.

I am not the slightest bit interested if a man is rich or poor, educated or ignorant nor in which way he casts his votes nor in the color of his skin.

If I can help him, then my ministry is available to him on the basis that he is a human being and, as such, deserves to be treated with dignity and respect.

Jesus Christ was not a politician. He was a Deliverer. God has called me to the ministry of deliverance.

UNTO THE HILLS

Unto the hills around do I lift up my longing eyes
O whence for me shall my salvation come, from whence arise
From God, the Lord, doth come my certain aid
From God, the Lord, Who heaven and earth hath made

He will not suffer that thy foot be moved: safe shalt thou be
No careless slumber shall His eyelids close, Who keepeth thee
Behold, He sleepeth not, He slumbereth ne'er
Who keepeth Israel in His holy care

Jehovah is Himself thy Keeper true, thy changeless Shade
Jehovah thy Defense on thy right hand Himself hath made
And thee no sun by day shall ever smite
No moon shall harm thee in the silent night

From every evil shall He keep thy soul, from every sin
Jehovah shall preserve thy going out, thy coming in
Above thee watching, He Whom we adore
Shall keep thee henceforth, yea, forevermore

C. H. Purday

CHAPTER 3

THE CHAPTER I DID NOT WANT TO WRITE

This chapter I didn't want to write. The exception to this statement is the contents of the very last part of the chapter which is revealed in due course. The reason for my reluctance is that there is little pleasure in recalling the most horrible and difficult period of my life. It is almost repulsive just thinking about it. That period of my life, however, has a most important and significant part in my story. Each time the Lord directs me to give my life story in one of our meetings, I know I have to tell this part. So in this book, I have to tell you of the worst days I have ever experienced. It would be more pleasant just to write about nice things, but it would not be the whole story. Life has valleys as well as mountains, negatives as well as positives. I have to tell you of **MY** long, lonesome valley, but I will also tell you how God miraculously brought me through what seemed to be a totally impossible situation. I pray that in relating these experiences, others who have similar problems may find some help and comfort.

After I had made my full commitment to God at the age of sixteen in early 1955, I quickly became involved in my local church. We had been raised Presbyterians, but my mother had changed to a little church which was both nearer and, she felt, much more spiritual. This small assembly was the Nazarene Church very close to our home. We had been attending this church for some time and it was natural, following my total dedication to God, that I should go to work for Him in that church.

The pastor was the Rev. George Brown who was a great friend to me. Although he did not preach Bible deliverance as I know it today, he nevertheless loved God with all his heart. He preached fervently on his beliefs as he knew them. The greatest single impression which he left upon my life was that, above all things, I should find the will of God and do it. I found this advice highly significant.

"The will of God" was his constant theme. To this day I lay great stress upon the necessity of individual Christians finding out God's perfect will for their lives.

Indeed, I rejoice that I am doing what God wants me to do. I want to do it even better, of course. I want to be more efficient. I work towards that end all the time, but the direction in which my life is flowing is the direction God wants for me. The joy of knowing that you are in God's will is beyond description. It brings tranquility which defies description. George Brown repeatedly urged his listeners to find God's will for their lives. I took him and God seriously on that issue. Soon after I was involved in the church, brother Brown was called to another church in Scotland. After some lengthy deliberations he decided to accept. Our church was then without a pastor for some time.

It was about this time that my troubles started and became gradually worse. A great spirit of confusion and darkness enveloped my impressionable young life. I was loathe to discuss my difficulties with others and suffered in silence. Things were made worse by the fact that my pastor was gone and I had no one to confide in.

Most of my ugly mental battles were caused by the horrifically negative preaching which I had to endure. The new pastor talked so much about "sanctification" and being holy that I felt more and more condemned. He seemed to know nothing about the fact that "righteousness is a gift." He would say such things as, "Have you prayed enough today?" "Have you read your Bible enough today?" "Have you witnessed to people today?" "If you are not doing these things, you could be the one holding up revival and people will go to hell as a result." I wanted to please God but I always fell short. I was entering into a nightmare because of the wrong preaching I was listening to. Had I been older I would probably have left that church. However, I was led to believe that the pastor was so holy and so right. So I saw no way out.

I had always been a happy-go-lucky type of person. In fact, one of my school reports carried these "remarks" from Mr. Cave, my teacher: "Lively but responsive." My mother laughed at the comment many, many times. I had been lively and happy. Now a spirit of depression, melancholy, confusion gradually came over me. Frankly, I did not know how to use God's Word against the devil. I did not know about the great principle of "Say So." (That was the title of a booklet I later wrote telling people how to stand on God's Word.) I did not know how to "Say So" against the devil. I did not know how to stand upon God's promises. I had not been taught these things. It's clear to me now that the devil tried to take my mind. I fought a terrible battle of fear, guilt, inferiority, and utter confusion.

Gradually, the clouds became darker and I became more miserable. It's horrible even to think about it as I write! Finally, it seemed as if all the depression and oppression in the world were put together in a steel band and that steel band was clasped over my forehead. I was in utter bondage beyond anything I can start to describe.

As I have told of this experience in various places, people have come to me afterwards saying that they had suffered the same thing. I am sure others did suffer so, but I also know that many who have said they did actually didn't. I know from the way they talk and the things they say. They may have had attacks of depression or fear. That is mild in comparison to what I felt. I am talking about going through a chamber of horrors. It was a nightmare. My head felt like a monumental weight on my shoulders. I lost all joy of living and became almost like a robot. Fear gripped me. I could see no way out. I even contemplated praying to the devil and asking him to leave me alone for a while. What a terrible thought, but it does reveal what condition I was in. All this made me physically exhausted. I went to bed early and still woke exhausted. All this time I was doing my level best to live for God. I was elected young people's leader in the church and then the young people's leader of all the churches in the country. I was now a member of the full church board. I was attending church, reading the Bible, and praying. Yet all that time I felt destitute in my spirit. I was miserable. Perhaps the biggest weight of all was the feeling of condemnation. I was always condemned. I lived in a negative world. If I did something, I would immediately feel wrong and condemned for doing it; yet I knew that if I left it undone, I would have felt equally guilty for not doing it.

The strange thing was that I always felt worse on a good bright, sunny day. Whether it was because the heat made me feel more tired and miserable or whether it was because everybody else, particularly other young people, seemed to be so happy and brightly dressed, emphasizing further, my own heaviness, I just do not know. I do know, however, that the brighter the day, the worse I felt.

How I kept my mind on my job in those days I will simply never know. I had left the lawyers and was now working in the Inglis Biscuit and Cake Bakery at Holywood Arches in the east end of Belfast. Each day seemed to get longer. Each day my mind was more tormented, I was ever conscious of my own thoughts. It seemed I couldn't relax. I was just not myself. It was a frightful experience. Oh, how I thank God for the ministry of deliverance and the emphasis on how to invoke God's power over the devil.

Things were getting worse for me then. I prayed as much as I could. Sometimes I prayed for hours until I was so exhausted that I would fall over the bed at which I was kneeling and fall fast asleep. When I awoke and realized what had happened, I'd feel more condemned than ever. I know what it was like to go for months and months doing my best to be a real Christian and never once to feel happy or relaxed, never once to feel the presence of God.

One day I walked down the corridor in the Inglis factory, into the main foyer beside the revolving doors. I was at the end of the road. I stopped, looked upward, and from my heart I cried, "Though God slay me, yet will I trust Him!" (Job 13:15) I desperately wanted to serve God. Many times I cried. I was so unhappy. The devil was making a total bid, not only to wreck my life but, above all, to keep me back from this great ministry of power and of faith which God had for me.

Let me remind you that the devil is out to destroy us, particularly during our formative years. In church I would stand up to lead a young people's meeting, or even to speak at it, with my heart breaking. I was in sorrow and despair. The mental torment was agonizing. I was not being hypocritical. I meant every word I told those young folk, even though I myself was passing through the valley of despair. The remarkable thing was the way God blessed the young people's department of that church during that terrible period. Many were saved and influenced for God. My internal battle, however, continued.

All this had been developing over a long period. By late '57 and early '58 things were pretty grim.

The only good I can see from the whole episode (nor is it inconsiderable) is the fact that, having gone through such darkness myself, I can now identify with others who have similar battles and help them through to total victory. If you have been or are going through anything like this, then know for sure that deliverance is there for you. It will come in two ways. First, the yoke of bondage will be broken and secondly, you will learn how to use the mighty Word of God in a powerful way against the devil.

By this time I was desperate. Something had to happen. I could not continue the way I was going.

God, glory to His name, was all the time preparing my deliverance for me. I have no doubt in my mind that what happened to me was a severe attack of the devil. It was certainly not God's work. He does good things. I learned a good many things from this experience, especially the secrets of faith in God and His power over Satan.

God works in mysterious ways and I want to share one of them with you. A gentleman called George McDade was totally unknown to me at that time. I had never heard of him in any way. As it turned out he only lived a few miles from my home, but he was an utter and total stranger to me and I to him. Soon, in God's providence, we would meet and because of this meeting, my present ministry of deliverance would be born.

George was not a preacher. He worked as a technician at Queens University in Belfast. George had no desire to be a preacher. He did have some evangelistic films though. I don't know how he originally came across them; but I do know that he had used them many times, showing them through an old and battered 16mm. projector. He also told me that he would never ask for bookings. He would never telephone a preacher and ask for an opening to show a film, but George still showed the films. Sometimes the projector would break down. In fact, oftimes it broke down, but George was a genius at making a quick repair and soon the machine was rolling again. If doors opened up he showed the films. If they didn't open up, he didn't try to open them. That is the way George McDade worked with the few old black and white films he had.

As I was praying desperately for deliverance or for something to happen, God started dealing with George in a very, very strong way. He could not understand it. He tried to shake off the feeling, but it would not go away. Over and over again, he was impressed with the word "Nazarene." He hadn't the slightest idea what it meant or what God was trying to say, if indeed it was God. He had never heard of the Nazarene church. He would open his Bible at random and it would fall at some Scripture using the word "Nazarene." He was baffled. Finally, he told his wife he was going out for a walk. He wanted to meditate upon all this and try to determine what it meant. He asked God to show him what it was he should know. He called on God as he walked, for further light.

Suddenly, after walking for quite a while, he came upon a little church. It was the one I attended and outside a notice said "Church of the Nazarene." He had never heard of it and although the word "Nazarene" fairly jumped out at him, he actually thought that it might be a Jewish Synagogue! He stopped to read the notice board. On it he found the name and address of the pastor. A new pastor had been installed to take over from George Brown. George McDade headed straight for the pastor's home which was not too far away. He knocked on the door and when the pastor came out, George said he had evangelistic films and would like to show one in the Nazarene church. This was the same George who never asked for bookings! He told me later he felt embarrassed standing there asking for a opening from a preacher he had neither met nor even heard of previously!

God moves in tremendous ways, His wonders to perform! It was all part of God's answer to my prayers of sorrow and desperation!

At that time, George McDade had no idea of the part he was playing in bringing this ministry into being. He had no inkling that he was helping to bring about my deliverance from this awful, oppressive yoke. The pastor simply said that he did not deal with films, but advised the stranger on his doorstep to contact his young people's leader. That was me. When George McDade talked to me, I explained how the acoustics in the church were not very good because of the low ceiling. I asked if he could come on a Wednesday evening, when nobody was there, for a trial showing. If things worked out, I told him we would give him a meeting. He said he didn't really think that was necessary, but he was happy to go along with my suggestion. George had no car, so my father drove me over to his house and we picked him and all his equipment up and headed back to the church. At the church we set up the projection gear. We were not there that day to actually view the film, but just to have a sound test for a few minutes. If everything was all right, we would then arrange a date for a service.

As I stood there waiting for George to throw the switch and commence the film, little did I realize that what would happen in the next few minutes would change my life dramatically and forever. It would also change the lives of tens of thousands of others.

The lights were put out, the projector started to roll and the opening music came pouring through. It was lively and exciting. Then five words flashed across the screen and they triggered something in my spirit. The words excited, blessed, and thrilled me. The words were the title of the film. "GOD IS A GOOD GOD!" I looked at them, blinked, swallowed my spittle, and was already able to see out there somewhere a new life of victory for me. "GOD IS A GOOD GOD." The words were music to my weary soul. Most people would say that that is elementary. Everybody knows that God is a good God. But that is not true. If it were true, why do we blame bad things on Him? Why do we say He sends sickness and poverty and other evils upon people? Why do we associate God so much with bad things? Why?

Yet it was not only the words. It was the enlightenment of my spirit as my eyes took in the words. In a flash, something happened. I could see that it was true. God is a good God! I felt I had received a message, a truth I had never had or understood before. I felt I needed to tell the whole world about this. Of course, I still had the "steel band" of oppression clasped tightly around my mind. I was not set free then. That was to come soon after but on that joyous night, a revelation came to me which still thrills me to the depths of my spirit. There is nothing worse than negative preaching. That is what I had been enduring. Some preachers actually do their best to arouse a guilt complex in their congregation. They specialize in 'Sin-consciousness!' The result is that their best members and the ones most sensitive to God are the most miserable. They are the first to feel guilty. To be absolutely honest, although I did not realize it then, the preaching I was exposed to was making my state of depression much worse. I actually remember praying one day, "Oh God, forgive me." Then I paused, "Lord I don't know what I need forgiveness for, but please forgive me anyhow." Negative preaching is a bane and a curse. It brings people into bondage.

Now everything was different for me. It's amazing what I saw in those few seconds while the title was on the screen. God is a good God. God wants to deliver people, to set them free, to turn them loose. I felt as if I was learning about the real Jesus and the real Gospel for the very first time.

Then a preacher was shown on the screen, and he announced he was going to preach on the subject "God is a good God." Did he preach it! He told how his life had been completely changed when he too had discovered the truth of God's goodness and of his great desire to set humanity free. If I was excited by the opening music and thrilled beyond words with the title, how can I ever describe my feelings as this man preached! I was beside myself! They were easily the most thrilling moments of my entire life up to then. This man preached with power. I had not been used to that. He preached with anointing. I had not been used to that either. He was in command of the situation. No begging, whining prayers. He talked to God as if he knew Him. And he did! This man was on fire! This man had something! And from the size of the crowd, it seemed to me that he was doing more for God accidentally than most men do on purpose!

His name was Oral Roberts. The end of the film was dramatic beyond words. I saw people come flocking down the aisles to be saved. Then Oral Roberts called the healing line. He laid hands on those people and God performed many notable miracles. When the film had run its 30 minute course and the lights were switched on, I was in a new world. Thank God for George McDade and thank God for Oral Roberts!

Something mighty had happened inside me. My spirit was alive. The hour of my deliverance from the mental yoke of bondage was also at hand. It happened like this.

Brother McDade came and showed a few of Brother Roberts' films in our meetings. The vast majority of people thought the films were great, although some objected. I was in no mood to worry about, nor even think about, objectors. I got George back for another meeting. He showed two films. The place was packed. I got up and thanked George and asked the people if they would like to see another film. They shouted "Amen!" Soon the third film was rolling. When it was over, I got up to close the meeting. The screen was mounted on the platform so I stood down below it and called somebody to close in prayer. THEN IT HAPPENED. Oh, thanks be to God a million times over that it happened!! The powerful anointing from the film and from Brother Roberts preaching permeated every cubic inch of the atmosphere! Soon the words of the man who was closing the meeting in prayer began to fade.

I stood there at the front of that little church looking up to God. All I knew about deliverance was what I had heard from these few films, but it was enough. In desperation, I cried to God. I remember my prayer. "Oh God, please deliver me, body, soul, mind, and spirit!" At that second it took place. The power of God, like a powerful bolt of lightning, struck me straight in my forehead. In an instant, the yoke, that strong terrible yoke, was

45

broken and I was utterly, completely, and gloriously free! Oh I was free, free, free!

I can never even start to describe that moment. I felt light. I felt happy. I felt the Spirit of God. I felt anointed. I felt love flowing in my heart.

Although I would have many more obstacles to fight and much criticism to endure before I would actually start preaching deliverance and praying for the sick as I do today, the main thing happened at that second.

The Bible says that the yoke shall be destroyed because of the anointing (Isaiah 10:27). My yoke was destroyed and I was free. I then had to learn how to keep my deliverance through standing on the Word of God. That knowledge comes about less dramatically than the original deliverance, but it is essential if the deliverance is to be maintained.

If you have never been through this glorious experience, you can be forgiven if you cannot understand why I was so excited that night; but that's why I still get so emotional and excited over my great deliverance.

Perhaps you are like the little girl who was playing hopscotch outside the prison when suddenly the gates swung open and a man came out, running and dancing and shouting, "I'm free! I'm free! I'm free!!!" The little girl stopped, looked up at him and said blandly, "What's the matter with you, I'm four!" She had never been in jail. There was no way she could appreciate what it was like to be free.

When you have been in bondage and God miraculously delivers you, it is so wonderful that you want to tell the world about it. More than that, you want to give your life to helping others to be delivered also. That is exactly what I am doing.

One more thing about Oral Roberts. At the time of this writing, Oral is now ninety-one years of age. I will be forever grateful for his obedience to the Lord, way back then, for preaching Bible deliverance. Of course, for many years I have been totally out of touch with the Oral Roberts Ministry. I cannot leave this subject without mentioning "Seed Faith." When Oral first started speaking about "Seed Faith," it seemed to me a new fresh way to talk about the giving of our tithes and offerings. However, after I moved to America and was here for a short while, I started seeing preachers on TV who were using "Seed Faith" as a money-making racket. It was utterly disgusting and it is still prevalent on US Christian TV today. I want nothing to do with such ungodly preaching and I have spoken out against it strongly on TV. We do not "buy" things from God. We cannot "bribe" God. We do not operate with God on a QUID PRO QUO basis. What we are to do is to TRUST God all the way.

WHEN NATURE WANTS A MAN

When Nature wants to drill a man
And thrill a man,
And skill a man,
When Nature wants to mould a man
To play the noblest part;
When she yearns with all her heart
To create so great and bold a man
That all the world shall praise--
Watch her method, watch her ways!
How she ruthlessly perfects
Whom she royally elects;
How she hammers him and hurts him
And with mighty blows converts him
Into trial shapes of clay
Which only Nature understands--
While his tortured heart is crying
And he lifts beseeching hands!--
How she bends, but never breaks,
When his good she undertakes....
How she uses whom she chooses
And with every purpose fuses him,
By every art induces him
To try his splendor out--
Nature knows what she's about.

(CONTINUED ON PAGE 58)

CHAPTER 4

OH GOD! I WANT TO SEE YOU IN ACTION!

Through my long journey in the valley of despair, I had continued to do my best to serve God. I attended every meeting I possibly could, and I rarely missed the special Sunday prayer meeting at eight o'clock in the morning. Only the faithful few attended this service and I was one of them. Many times I prayed in desperation, "Oh God, I want to see you in action!" I was not merely upset because of my own battles, but because of the sad lack of God's power in the meetings. Very, very little seemed to be happening. We went through the motions of a meeting, but I doubt if anybody there actually expected anything special to happen. Signs and wonders never took place and very, very rarely did anybody ever inquire about salvation. This was a wretched way for a church to operate and I was extremely dissatisfied. At that time, I knew nothing of God's great power of the baptism of the Holy Spirit or of praying for the sick. When I called upon God to "see Him in action," I was verbalizing the longings of my inner man without really knowing what I was asking for. I didn't know how God could or would manifest Himself, but I longed for a demonstration of His mighty power.

Our services were so far removed from what Jesus did in the four Gospels and from the works of the followers of Jesus, as recorded in the book of Acts, that it was pitiable.

Even though I, myself, was in the midst of a great personal battle, I realized something was seriously wrong with the thinking and attitude of other believers. They did not seem remotely interested nor concerned whether God manifested Himself or not. I wanted to get back to the Bible. I had already been delivered. I had seen the order of the Acts of the Apostles in a new way. I therefore determined that nothing would stop me from having God's great power in my life to do for my world what the young church had done for theirs.

This, then started me on the road to get God's anointing mightily upon my life. When I look back now, I can see just what a road it has been! I have had many victories, but what battles there have been! If a person is not prepared to give up everything and seek God single-heartedly, through thick and thin, he can forget about God's power.

Although our Lord wants His power to be used in a greater way than is evident in the world today, He does not give it cheaply. It costs to get God's power and it costs to keep it. You can have an empty prayer room and mount the pulpit to criticize those praying for the sick, but you MUST have an occupied private prayer room if you are going to come down from the pulpit and heal the sick.

I have not had the formal education that most preachers have had. I have never been to Bible school. I often tell of a particular night several years ago when I was passing through Glasgow, Scotland and I was put up for the night in a Bible college. I didn't pay for my board that night. I slept on it! I don't really think that hindered me from going to Bible School! Such an experience just did not come my way. The same applies to a university. That didn't come my way either. I am not, in any way saying this to indicate that I am against these places of higher learning. Of course not! I am merely telling it as it happened to me.

I felt my main concern was to seek God for both His mighty power and His directive for my life. I could increasingly feel His call. I knew He wanted me to do His work. I knew more and more that the only ministry for me was the ministry of miracles, the Holy Spirit, and the power of the Holy Spirit. I became unbelievably restless, frustrated, and dissatisfied. It would seem that when a young man becomes desperate for God's power and when he has just received a mighty deliverance himself, that everybody would be on his side. Everybody, that is, in the church world. How very far from the truth that is. Circumstances seem to crowd in on you, and people you thought were your friends become angry with you. They turn against you and criticize you fiercely. It's all part of the price to be paid. Indeed, that early opposition was nothing compared to what I have faced since. Still, it made no difference to my spirit and my determination. If it had any effect, it was the opposite to what the devil intended. It made me more determined!

I wanted to get to KNOW God. I wanted to know Him privately, personally, and intimately. I wanted to talk with Him and get answers. I wanted to know that I was carrying out His wishes and commands. I wanted to be effective, to be fruitful, and to see things happen.

Now that I have come through much of all that seeking and now that God's power rests upon my life, I am so thankful that God helped me to be faithful and to seek Him unreservedly. I simply cannot bear the thought of no miracles and no mighty deliverances; it is enough to upset me. How some men, who say they are called of God, can sail along with nothing happening and God not on the scene baffles me completely.

What good is a mathematician if he cannot add and subtract?

What good is a beautiful grocery store if they have no food on the shelves?

What good is a brand new luxury trawler if it cannot catch fish?

What good is a center-forward if he cannot score goals?

And, I ask you, what good is a preacher without God's power?

And what good is a church which has degenerated into a social club and which cannot set the people free?

I wanted God's power above every other thing upon the face of the earth. I wanted it for God's glory and to do His bidding. So I gave myself to the Word of God and prayer.

I was so naive, so ignorant of a real Bible ministry that I had to "unlearn" many old traditional things before I could start to fully appreciate the liberating truths of God's Word.

So it was a long, long time before God's great power would come into my life; but in the intervening years, He dealt with me gloriously. He gave me several great miracles and spoke to me on different occasions.

Looking back, I am very grateful for all the wondrous things God did for me during those years of seeking His face and power. However, my heart was not satisfied until He came to me and told me that my hour had come. Nevertheless, I realize God had to deal gently and patiently with me. When a man decides to give up everything in order to have God's power in his life, he has to learn many lessons; and the journey is long and difficult.

In the next chapter I will tell you of the way in which God finally came to me in the way I had always sought and longed for.

Meantime, I want to share with you some of the experiences that happened to me during my years of searching. These experiences are very important to my story.

I left my job in the bakery and launched into full-time service for the Lord. I knew it was God's time for me to do this, but that was about all I knew. God honored the move and provided for me supernaturally. I continued praying. I would walk up and down the attic of my mother's home pleading for God's power. Then a wonderful thing happened, which greatly encouraged me.

I was holding meetings in a town some miles from Belfast. As I locked my mini-bus and started toward the door of the church, I became keenly aware of the presence of God in a distinct way. This unusual feeling of "awe" stayed with me throughout the service and on the journey home. I could not understand it, except to know that it was a beautiful presence. God's presence seemed to envelop me. The next day I was sitting in my home when, suddenly, God spoke to me. Previously I had had experiences when God had guided and directed me to do certain things, but this time He actually spoke. Deep inside my spirit, I heard from heaven. I shall never forget that thrilling moment. Here are His words:

"Everything is all right now. Your ministry will begin to open up and I will supply all the anointing you need to carry out your work."

God's presence filled the room. I didn't know what to do. My first thought was this, "What if an angel had appeared before my physical eyes and spoke those words to me?" I don't know why that thought came to me; but I do know, without planning it and as a reflex action, I found myself dismissing the thought! I didn't want an angel. I felt that it would not be as convincing as the voice I had just heard!

After a while, I put on my coat and went for a walk. I didn't know what all this would mean in the future, but I realized I had had a great experience which few men have had. I had heard from God. He had spoken to me. As I walked, I felt humble, peaceful, and contented. "Everything is all right now." What peaceful words. "Your ministry will now begin to open up." Those words proved to be so correct in the months and years that lay immediately ahead. "I will supply all the anointing you need to carry out your work." That was what I wanted, power commensurate to my calling. God's call to set the people free was pounding upon my spirit more and more, and I knew I needed a great anointing to effectively do what God was asking me to accomplish for Him.

God's words were both inspirational and prophetic, but I still had a long way to go before He would tell me that my hour had finally arrived. In fact, I still had years to wait. Even so, those years were filled with outstanding successes in the Kingdom of God.

My ministry did begin to open up. I published some tracts and people wrote asking for copies. They wrote telling me how the literature had blessed them. I got a typewriter and answered the letters. More letters and prayer requests came flooding in. Calls came asking me to hold meetings around Northern Ireland. Then requests came from England, Scotland, and Wales.

Let me take you back just a little. After my great deliverance, one of the very first things I did was to go into the streets and hold open-air meetings. I still did not have the baptism of the Holy Spirit. I was being severely criticized even for preaching about healing, but how God blessed those meetings.

One Sunday evening, after I had spoken to a great crowd, I asked all those who wanted to accept Christ as their personal Saviour to leave the crowd and come and stand beside me at the microphone. Twenty-eight souls moved forward. The next Sunday nineteen responded to the call. I was only preaching what I had learned from the film and God was honoring my boldness and faith.

When I finally stopped the open air meetings because the evenings were getting too dark, there was a public outcry. Men came along and rigged up flood lights, and the police came to keep things under control. Hundreds were reached through those wonderful street meetings. Such was their success that street meetings continued as part of my ministry for quite some time.

One day as I was walking towards the place where we were holding these street meetings, I found myself walking across a vacant lot. Evidently something had been on it at one time, but whatever it was had been bombed during the war. Now it was vacant. Suddenly I stopped. Two seconds previously, I didn't know what I was going to do. There and then I called upon God. "Oh God," I said, "Reserve this spot for me for your glory!" Then I went on my way.

Later on, I entered full-time service. The ministry was opening up. I was busier than ever and had just returned from marvelous meetings in England.

As I was walking along Belfast's York Road, a lovely building was almost completed right on the spot where I had prayed my prayer. God was about to answer that prayer of long ago.

I could feel the Spirit of God urging me to buy that building. I had no money, no organization, and no denomination. I didn't even understand how to go about it. But God's "urgings" became stronger. Finally, I telephoned the real-estate agents. "I would like to rent an office in that new building on York Road" I said. I felt that the increase in my activity justified having an office. I had been using my mother's parlour and it was now bulging at the seams. "Sorry," replied the agent, "we are not renting any offices. We are selling the entire building. It is not for rent." I asked him the price. "Nine thousand pounds," he said. Today that may not seem a very large amount, but in 1961 it was huge. I was young, and inexperienced and, it is worth pointing out, I had no money whatsoever.

I thanked him and hung up the phone. What would I do now?

I thought a great deal about that building. God didn't want me to rent an office. His dealings with me were not along those lines. I knew I had to buy that building. It seemed a gigantic step and, unquestionably, it was, but God was telling me to do it. I knew I had His mind on the matter.

Well-meaning friends sometimes become afraid when a man sets out to obey God. Believe me, the man has no option! He has to obey God or his life is as good as finished! People were afraid for me. Others laughed, but I was never more serious in all my life. This building was only three streets away from where I was born. I was operating in my own area, which is sometimes the hardest place. Still, what good was it to ask God for His guidance and then not to act upon His revealed will? I decided to act.

I went to the real-estate agent's office. They gave me a nice chair and asked what my business was.

"Do you see that building on York Road?"

"Yes."

"I want to buy it!"

"You want to buy it?"

"Yes."

"All right. Pull your chair over and give me some details."

I gave the man my name and address. I was only twenty-one years of age. I was obeying God.

A remarkable thing happened during our conversation. I did not plan it. It just happened this way. After asking me several questions, the man then looked at me and said, "Who are your bankers?" What a question. I had no bankers. I could easily have carried everything I had in my inside coat pocket.

At that instant, something tickled my throat. I promise you I didn't plan it, arrange it, or even pray for it. It started tickling. Everybody has that happen at one time or another. Admittedly it doesn't usually happen when you are buying a £9,000 building without any money, and you have just then been asked who your bankers are. That's when it happened to me. I started coughing. I had a friend with me and he just stared at me. I felt embarrassed as my coughing got worse. Finally, I reached for my handkerchief and tears started rolling down my cheeks. Right there, in the office, did I ever have a fit of coughing! The man kindly waited. I finally got some control of myself and turned to the man. "Excuse me please," I said. "It is all right," he answered. "What were you saying?" I enquired. "Who are your bankers?" he asked again. Right then, it happened again. The tickling started and got worse. I turned away from the desk and coughed and coughed and coughed. My friend was still staring. I turned back after a few spluttering, embarrassing moments.

"Excuse me please," I said again.

"It's all right," he replied.

"What were you saying?" I asked

"Who are your bankers?" He replied.

For the third time it happened. It happened exactly as I am telling it. I didn't arrange the tickling, but tickle my throat it did. Wow! Did it tickle! I turned aside again. I coughed and coughed and coughed. My friend just kept staring. I assure you I wasn't acting. I was coughing. Genuinely coughing! After regaining partial control, I turned again to the patient real-estate agent. "Excuse me please," I said, "It's all right," he said. "What were you saying?" I asked. "Oh, it's all right," he replied. "I'll get that information later!" My throat quit tickling and I signed on the dotted line.

The ball was now rolling. I had just committed myself to buying a building. All I needed was the money. I needed more than £10,000, £9,000 for the building plus legal costs and some work which needed completing on the inside of the building.

God undertook this task in a marvelous way. That building became a "beehive" of activity. It housed Faith Tabernacle, where multitudes found deliverance. There were offices, a printing department, and a telephone ministry.

It wasn't easy to get the money. It was long and difficult. It seemed I had discouragement after discouragement, but I refused to lie down.

That building and the one next to it which we also bought were fully paid for and debt free.

WHEN NATURE WANTS A MAN

When Nature wants to take a man
And shake a man
And wake a man;
When Nature wants to make a man
To do the Future's will;
When she tries with all her skill
And she yearns with all her soul
To create him large and whole....
With what cunning she prepares him!
How she goads and never spares him,
How she whets him and she frets him
And in poverty begets him....
How she often disappoints
Whom she sacredly anoints,
With what wisdom she will hide him,
Never minding what betide him
Though his genius sob with slighting
And his pride may not forget!
Bids him struggle harder yet.
Makes him lonely
So that only
God's high messages shall reach him
So that she may surely teach him
What the Hierarchy planned.
Though he may not understand
Gives him passions to command--
How remorselessly she spurs him,
With terrific ardor stirs him
When she poignantly prefers him!

(CONTINUED ON PAGE 66)

CHAPTER 5

THE VISION FROM GOD

I would now like to talk about the vision which God put into my being as a young man. I believe it started to take hold in my spirit when we lived in Knockview off the Doagh Road in Newtownabbey, just outside of Belfast in Northern Ireland. I was serving God. I was living for Him and preaching the Gospel with a very young family. God came to me and started to deal with me in very, very powerful ways. I distinctly remember staying up late, night after night until one, two, three, four o'clock in the morning. I was literally walking up and down our living room and calling upon the Almighty as He was showing me what He wanted for my life in the days to come; and He was revealing it bit by bit, little by little. In fact, it was so intense that in addition to my other duties of preaching and teaching and so forth, I was literally giving myself to prayer. I remember I would come home from Sunday service and ofttimes not even come out of my room until the mid-week service. I would be calling upon the Lord, literally day and night.

It would take weeks and sometimes months for one part of the vision to really become clear. Then no time after that part was clear, another part of the vision would come and it would take weeks or months. It would grow. It would be like giving birth to something. It was bit by bit. Sometimes it was hard and sometimes it wasn't so hard. This lasted for, I don't know, a year or two. It was just very, very powerful. It ended up by God showing me what He wanted, for my life and ministry, several outreaches and several buildings and that I was to use them for the glory of God. I knew, even though I was a young preacher, I had heard from Heaven.

For example, I remember seeing in my spirit, with clarity, the sanctuary that He wanted us to have. It was large, and rectangular, and there was a kitchen attached to it. I could see that clearly. Of course all of this was coming as a surprise to me, because at the beginning I was a traveling evangelist and now God was showing me this. It was most unusual. Other things too, were coming to me bit by bit until I felt the vision was complete. Many times even during the day when I was driving, the dealings of God would continue but especially when I was on my own in those early hours of the morning seeking and calling on the Almighty.

After a while several outreaches would become clear, that He wanted me to do. So I started to look for land, to build on. I went back to my good friend John Crowe, from whom we had bought Faith Tabernacle on the York Road in Belfast. He told me that he had some acres at Glengormley, just outside Belfast, and I could have those. I did want those acres but my lawyer and the planning department told me I could never build on that land; all of that is quite a story. I bought them anyway and then we bought more acres from a local farmer until we had several acres to build on. I eventually got planning permission. In fact, we did build the first building and part of the second building. However, as a young preacher on fire for God and absolutely filled with the power of the Holy Ghost and as I started to verbalize this vision, I could never have anticipated the evil that rose up against me. This opposition was from men whose hearts were filled with demonic forces to try to stop and destroy me. I remember one man in particular who said to me, "My mission in life is to destroy your mission in life." I remember another man who said, "I'll blacken you where ever I will go." I never did any of the two of them one bit of harm, and yet Satan was rising up in a very powerful way.

In spite of all opposition, I was determined to go through with the plan and vision at Glengormley with no intention to move to America even though I loved America very much and still do, even more in fact. Then God changed it in that remarkable encounter in Florida when I was in the mall in Orlando. God changed it. I never thought of it. What was He doing? I guess it was like the Apostle Paul when he said, "I turn to the gentiles." Or was it like what Jesus said, "If they don't receive you wipe the dust from off your feet." Whatever it was, God made it clear that He was changing location from Glengormley to Florida. It didn't all become clear in an instant and, of course, I kept obeying God as He opened doors.

I knew, of course, He transferred us to America. I remember, not too long after being in America for a while, I received a phone call from Ireland. The caller was Bobby Busby, a very dear friend from a town called Dungannon. He had a car business in the town and was well known as RJ Busby Motors. Bobby was a wonderful friend and supporter and helped financially in many ways. He was a humble and godly man. In fact the first time I ever heard of him, I was standing behind a curtain about to preach in an auditorium in Dungannon when somebody brought me a note from Bobby. I would get to know him later in person. Written in green ink, I will always remember what it said, "There was a man they called him mad, the more he gave the more he had." Bobby Busby was an outstanding Christian. He called me from Dungannon while I was in Florida and took me by surprise. In fact, he took me by such surprise that I was in a state of absolute shock. "Leslie," he said, "I know things have been very rough and people have fought you. But tell me Leslie, did God lead you away, or did you just get tired and you up and ran away from all the troubles, battles, and accusations?" From hearing this, I was in shock. It never once struck my mind to either run away or to leave Ireland. I was going to fulfill the call of God and do what God had called me. But God had changed me. God had changed the whole thing and brought me to America. It's not that I didn't love America. Before all this and during all this and different periods of time, I had amazing offers to come to America.

Offers Of Ministry

I remember one church in Rockford, Illinois, about an hour outside of Chicago, which made me an unbelievable offer. They had a large church, about a thousand members. At that time, many years ago, they were going to give me a thousand dollars a week. They had their own television bus, their own radio station, their own school, but God said no.

Then there was a big church in Houston, Texas with 5,000 members. The pastor asked me to become a co-pastor. He would speak in the mornings and I would speak in the evenings. I said no and now God is sending me to Kissimmee where there is nobody, but it was God so I went. Of course people fought us, the papers wrote against us, but they were all wrong.

I remember two men in particular, TL Osborn and Norvel Hayes. They had the witness in their hearts, loud and clear, that I was obeying God and that I should not do anything else but obey God. It was really a magnificent witness. In fact, TL Osborn looked at me and said "Leslie, I perceive that God is with you."

During that period of the vision, I saw that we would have a large sanctuary. I saw that we would have our own television facilities. I saw that we would have our own printing facilities. I saw that we would have a remarkable and wonderful Bible college. I saw that we would have a beautiful dining facility and other things too. I announced these things; it was for Glengormley. God wanted it. But do you know what happened? God moved me as people fought. I will never know the full details other than I obeyed God. But the vision that was for Glengormley is presently being fulfilled in Florida. We have that magnificent sanctuary and indeed it has a kitchen, right beside it. Although we have turned that into a "Reformation Room" (part of the Antique Bible Museum) because we have another kitchen in another building. We have our own television facilities, not just that we are on television but because we have our own television production. Our program is seen in all fifty states of the union, every Province of Canada, foreign countries, and of course by internet all over the world live. We have our own printing and print notes by the tens of thousands to give away free. We have an amazing Bible college. In fact, people can either come in person, or they can watch live on the internet around the world or later on get CD's or DVD's and join in the teaching. And do we ever have a dining facility? It is like a five star restaurant. One of the most beautiful dining facilities that you could ever imagine. Every single service is followed by wonderful fellowship and delicious food, and the food is always complimentary.

So I have the joy of knowing that not only did I obey God but I am obeying God. Not only was I in God's will but I am in God's will. When God sent me from Ireland to America, though I love America, I am repeating what I said before, I did not come just because of my love for the country otherwise I would have gone before to those lucrative offers. But I did go when God spoke to me. I am seeing things done wonderfully for His glory. We have a magnificent Antique Bible Museum, and we are building a marvelous Tabernacle-In-The-Wilderness as part of our Christian education outreach. All together, the thrill of my life is not only to be in God's will but to pursue God's will and pursue it fervently. I have done that for almost sixty years, to fulfill His will upon my life. The truth is this: I don't care who says what, who criticizes me, or what lies they tell about me on television, in the newspaper, or anywhere else. I am a man on fire for God with the love of God in my soul, and I am in sweet obedience to His will. I was yesterday, last month, last year, ten years ago, twenty years ago, and thirty years ago. All this I say for the honor and glory of God. I realize in ourselves we are nothing, but He gives us the grace to follow His wonderful will and His wonderful purposes. It's terrific to have a vision. You can be sure when you have a vision that you are going to have opposition, but it is terrific to see the enabling of God to carry out the vision even when God changes location. That really is something.

THE MOVING OF THE LORD

It reminds me, of course, when David went up against a certain enemy and he won. Then when the enemy came again, David was going to employ the same tactics. This time God said, "No, wait until you hear the going of the sound in the mulberry trees." The end purpose was the same. God wanted victory but God had a new direction, a new tactic. As Vep Ellis, my late good friend, wrote these wonderful words, "Let us determine in our hearts the way God's moving and move with God."

I am so pleased that so many thousands came to Christ in our meetings in Ireland. Many were healed and blessed; and we have heard from very many people by email and with wonderful, encouraging, and comforting words. People see how strong I am in God's will, and the fact that I did right and obeyed God. I was particularly thankful for the constant encouragement by Pastor Willie Dick, who had the witness so strong that I did what God had told me to do and am carrying out His purposes. Whether it was in Glengormley or Florida or Africa, it made no difference. I was going to obey God. It just happens to be that God is very good in allowing us to carry it out and live in beautiful sunny Florida.

When Nature wants to name a man
And fame a man
And tame a man;
When Nature wants to shame a man
To do his heavenly best....
When she tries the highest test
That her reckoning may bring--
When she wants a mighty king!--
How she reins him and restrains him
So his body scarce contains him
While she fires him
And inspires him!
Keeps him yearning, ever burning
For a tantalising goal--
Lures and lacerates his soul.
Sets a challenge for his spirit,
Draws it higher when he's near it--
Makes a jungle, that he clear it;
Makes a desert, that he fear it
And subdue it if he can--
So doth Nature make a man.
Then, to test his spirit's wrath
Hurls a mountain in his path--
Puts a bitter choice before him
And relentless stands o'er him.
"Climb, or perish!" so she says....
Watch her purpose, watch her ways!

(CONTINUED ON PAGE 74)

CHAPTER 6

COMING TO AMERICA

I want to describe the amazing, glorious, and even supernatural way that God led me and my family to live in and minister in the United States of America.

I have always loved America, but I had absolutely no plans ever to actually go and live in America. I remember when I was a little boy sitting at my father's feet. He was a master accordionist and he would play "The Stars & Stripes Forever." I loved that piece of music. I would look up and say, and I said it many times, "What's that one called daddy?" I remember him stopping and looking down, "That one is called 'The Stars & Stripes Forever.' It's about America and America is a wonderful country and don't you ever let anyone ever tell you anything different."

My father believed in free enterprise and the spirit of entrepreneurship. He was a wonderful man in every way and there is no doubt that he helped to create in me a tremendous love for America. But I had no plans to move to America. I was going to obey God whether it was Belfast or Bangladesh. This, I guess, can be proved by the fact that I had turned down amazing offers to go to America and preach there. I remember one particular offer that came from a big church not too far from Chicago, Illinois. This church had a large congregation. It had its own radio station, not merely on the radio, but they owned the radio station. They had a huge television truck. They had a Bible college, and they wanted me to come and be the pastor. The home they were providing was magnificent with a huge swimming pool. They were giving me a phenomenal salary and everything, as they say, was "laid on" to move from "bomb-wearied" Belfast to this beautiful place. Everything was perfect in the natural. I turned it down because the Holy Spirit would not let me, and I didn't even think anything more about it.

There was another occasion when the pastor of a 5,000 member church in Houston, Texas asked me to become his co-pastor. He would preach in the morning and I would preach in the evening. In fact, they actually had a satellite church and traveled between the two by helicopter. I turned that down also because it just wasn't of the Lord. So I was prepared to do everything God wanted me to do in Ireland. I had already won thousands of people to the Lord. God had blessed the ministry in an incredible way. Everybody knew about it from one end of Ireland to the other.

Then suddenly, totally and completely out of the blue, without me having one thought towards it, the Holy Spirit changed everything. Of course the question has to be asked, why? Well only God, I suppose, can answer that. I do know that Jesus said that there may come a time when you have to wipe the dust off your feet. Paul one time changed course and said, "From now on I go to the gentiles" (Acts 18:6). What was in God's mind? I don't know. Certainly, we were being fought, unbelievably not only from without but from within. People in the ministry were trying to steal it and various things.

Anyway, now back to the story about how God actually did lead us. One day I was sitting in my home in Ben Madigan Heights in Belfast, Northern Ireland when the phone rang. I had no idea who was calling. In fact, it was my good friend Reverend Dan Beller from the great International Pentecostal Holiness Church in Tulsa, Oklahoma, just down the street from Oral Roberts University. I had known Dan for a long time. He told me he was going on a trip to the Holy Land and asked if Maureen and I would fly to Tulsa and take his Sunday morning and evening services. I consented and asked our secretary Joan, when she was booking the tickets, if she would book it on the way home coming through Orlando, so that we would spend a few days rest there and enjoy Disney World and so forth and then back to Ireland. I never thought anything differently. So we went to Dan Beller's and came to the Orlando, Kissimmee area, the Disney World area. Then something absolutely unbelievable happened.

THE HAND OF GOD

We stopped at a little kiosk that was just beside the Holiday Inn on Highway 192 in Kissimmee to pick up some brochures about the tourist attractions of the area. After grabbing a bunch of material, we sat in the car in the parking lot looking at this material. Then I discovered that I had also picked up a real-estate magazine. So as Maureen was looking though some brochures, I was looking through this real-estate magazine. Lo and behold a church was for sale. Of course, I had no interest in it but if you're a preacher and there is a church for sale it grabs your interest. I suppose if you are a barber and you are in a foreign country, you would like to see how the barbers operate. Well this intrigued me but it didn't mean anything. It said it was on Ingram Street in Kissimmee but that was it. So we left the parking lot and started to drive. Lo and behold just down the street was Ingram Street. So at the last second, having discovered it, I just pulled in. I cannot tell you how unbelievably causal all this was, without the slightest, remotest idea of what God was about to do. We pulled in there and there was a carpenter working on the church. There were two buildings, a church and a second building. He was working there and we fell into conversation with him. I asked, "Is this place for sale?" He said, "Actually no, it's recently been bought by Mr. Miller." And he said, "We are converting it into apartments." "In fact," he said, "I already have this second building almost complete, and tomorrow I will start on the sanctuary to turn it into apartments." I said, "Oh, ok." I was about to leave and then he said, "Mr. Miller is really close here, just around the corner. Why don't you say hi?" So we did since we were heading that way anyway.

We stopped, and he had a beautiful store. Maureen looked around the store while I said hi to Mr. Miller. We fell into conversation, shook hands, wished each other the best, and then I left. I never had another thought about that church. It never came back into my mind. We went to the Fashion Square Mall on Colonial in Orlando. Maureen went round and round the mall. She loved the malls and still does. I walked a little bit and looked in a book store, the usual things.

Then something happened to me. It was as if all the mental battles in the world came together at one time. It was as if someone reached inside my being and pulled my nervous system out of joint. And I walked in what could be called such depression, such spiritual warfare. I was battling something and I had no idea in the world what it was. I continued walking and, of course, resisting the devil the best I could. I remember I walked out to our rental car, stayed there a few minutes, came back in again, and this thing got worse and worse. I was fighting and battling. In fact, Maureen told me at one point she actually saw me, but I didn't see her. She kind of went the other way, because she knew something was going on. She could read me that well. Finally, after a protracted period, I burst out with these words to the Lord, of course silently within myself, "Oh God, every time you speak to me I try to obey you immediately. And I am not obeying this time because I don't know what you are saying." I had switched from believing it was the devil, and now I began to think that this was God trying to get through to me. The moment I made that statement, instantly, the voice of God shot back and said, "Go buy that church. It's yours." And I said two words, having no idea of the ramifications or consequences, "Yes Lord!"

As soon as I said it, 1,000 pounds of weight was lifted off my shoulders. I felt free and happy and rejoiced again. I went looking for Maureen, got hold of her and said, "Let's go." She asked, "Where are we going?" I said, "We are going to buy that church." She said, "What?" We were about to leave to go back to Ireland (it was just a real short couple of days). So we drove back, not to the church but to the store, which was sort of around the corner from the church. We walked in and there was Mr. Miller. He looked at me with utter amazement and literally started to cry. Tears welled up in his eyes. I looked at him and said, "Mr. Miller, are you all right?" He said, "Yes, let me tell you a story." He said, "I called my father, who is a retired Church of the Nazarene preacher in North Carolina, and we talked about you. I talked to him about this Irish preacher." And he said that his father said to him, "You know something, God wants that preacher to have that church." I was astounded. I was utterly amazed to put it mildly. So I said, "The Lord has spoken to me about this church too." "Well," he said, "let's do something about it." So we went back around to the church. The carpenter was still working. Mr. Miller sent the carpenter to get a legal form. He brought it back. Remember we are total strangers up to that day. Then Mr. Miller asked the 64,000 dollar question, "How much are you going to put down for this church?" Of course, we didn't have anything: no money, no green card, no American citizenship, nothing. What am I doing buying a church in America? I was obeying God Almighty. I said to Maureen, in a whispered voice, "How much have we got?" She said, "a hundred dollars." So I said rather strongly and boldly, "Mr. Miller, I will put down a hundred dollars." "Right," he said, "I will take it." We signed the forms and we left.

It wasn't that long till we were flying back to Ireland. We owned a church in America and we would have to pay it off. I didn't know what to do with the church. As a matter of fact, I asked my good friend John Williamson in Toronto, Canada if he would pray about moving to Florida; because I had just bought a church and didn't know what to do with it since I was ministering in Ireland. John quickly told me that it wasn't God's will for him. So I was left with the church.

So we arrived back in Ireland. Even up to that point, I never thought that I would be moving to America. After a while, we came back to America and then God started to bless as we held some services. The first Sunday morning we had three people. On the fourth Sunday, just three Sundays later, there were more than 150 people. It was absolutely miraculous. Then God was showing me clearly that it was totally His will that "I" take care of that church! I was flabbergasted!

I remember just one other thing too: I can't exactly remember the timeline but on one of my visits back to Ireland, I was walking up the left-hand aisle of the church to stand at the front row to get ready to preach when God lifted the whole thing off of me relating to Ireland. I would still love the people, I would still be a blessing to them, but somebody else would have to be in leadership because God was transferring me from Ireland to the United States of America.

Obeying God

All of my life I have lived by this principle, OBEY GOD. I cannot emphasize enough the importance of these words in my life, to obey God. Of course, after you obey God then others will put their own supposition or application on why you did such and such, not realizing that you too don't have all the answers. It's merely that you obeyed your Heavenly Master. It's simply fantastic to be in the center of God's will.

WHEN NATURE WANTS A MAN

Nature's plan is wondrous kind
Could we understand her mind ...
Fools are they who call her blind.
When his feet are torn and bleeding
Yet his spirit mounts unheeding,
All his higher powers speeding
Blazing newer paths and fine;
When the force that is divine
Leaps to challenge every failure
And his ardor still is sweet
And love and hope are burning
In the presence of defeat....
Lo, the crisis! Lo, the shout
That must call the leader out.
When the people need salvation
Doth he come to lead the nation....
Then doth Nature show her plan
When the world has found--a man!

Angela Morgan

CHAPTER 7

PROVISION

Many years ago, when I was still a very young man and still living in St. Vincent Street off the Shore Road in Belfast, I had a remarkable experience with God. I am sure I was still in my teens at the time, probably late teens, and my custom was to get up and have an hour's prayer before going to work. This particular morning, I got up really early and did not want to disturb anyone else, so I tiptoed down the stairs in order to have my time with God. By the way, I need to say that I put great value on my time with God, my quiet time; and I have continued doing that for over fifty years, to meet with God in a special way each day. Even though, of course, we can talk to Him if we are driving in the middle of heavy traffic. But that special time is something else.

This particular morning would be very dramatic in my life. Obviously, I had no idea what was about to happen, but God had a certain plan for me. As in the Old Testament when God would show up and do something special and the people would raise up an altar, or a pillar, to remember how God appeared and gave them certain instructions, so I am recording what happened to me that day.

At the bottom of the stairs I turned into what we called the kitchen, although it was more like a living room. As I was tiptoeing very quietly, I glanced up at the wall for some reason and saw a picture with a text on it. It had been there for years and I knew it well, since I was the one who had bought it for my mother all those years ago. It was a text with a scene around it. It read, *"But my God shall supply all your need, according to his riches in glory, by Christ Jesus"* (Philippians 4:19).

Now that verse can be a blessing to all of us, but something most extraordinary happened to me that morning. It was as if that verse jumped off that picture and fastened onto my spirit. Then, it absolutely filled my being. It was as if it filled every part of me from the crown of my head to the soles of my feet. My whole body, as well as my spirit and soul, was filled with the knowledge of this tremendous promise, that God was going to supply all my needs. It so overwhelmed me that I hardly knew what to do with it. But the surprising thing was it didn't go away. It stayed with me for about 10 days, filling my being with exhilaration, joy, and blessing. I didn't realize, right at that time, what God was doing. He was giving me a promise for my life time, a promise for my ministry. Of course, I have been tested many times financially but now all these years later I can testify, "It's true!" God supplies all our needs especially and obviously when we learn to fully trust Him. It is terrific to trust Him and by His grace, I shall continue to trust Him until I see Him face to face. I must emphasize that this was something special. It was rare and powerful. I knew, as a young boy in Northern Ireland, that God Almighty had come on the scene and filled my being with His presence and His promise and it would hold true. How wonderful to know that it would hold TRUE all of my life.

From that time, of course, God has met my needs in glorious ways, some more dramatic than others. I would like to list just a few of the great miracles that God has performed. However, before I do I would like to tell an interesting story about God meeting our needs.

Several years ago when we were already in Faith Tabernacle on the York Road in Belfast, a dramatic happening took place. The demands were very great financially at the beginning of the month, and we didn't know how the needs were going to be met. Then somebody noticed a little old lady, dressed all in black. She came in the front door, during the day when there was no service going on. When somebody from upstairs went down to greet her, she was gone. They looked in every direction, but there was nobody around except an envelope sitting on the little desk. When we opened it, there was a hundred pounds inside. What a tremendous blessing. We rejoiced over the little lady in black, but after a while forgot about her. Then again we had tremendous needs and again the little lady in black showed up. My father noticed her while he was printing for us upstairs. I went downstairs but she was gone. I looked in every direction but there was nobody around, except for an envelope with a hundred pounds. This happened for a number of months. Somebody always got a glimpse of her; but by the time we arrived downstairs, there would be nobody there except for the hundred pounds. You talk about rejoicing. It was amazing! It was wonderful! She became known to all of us in the ministry as "the little lady in black." Then we came to a certain month where the needs were great again at the beginning of the month. And I remember thinking to myself, "Praise God, 'the little lady in black'." She had been doing it every month up to that point, for several months. Here's what happened. She never appeared again, not one more time. I didn't mean to do it, but subconsciously I had allowed her to become my source instead of the channel. I was still believing God but in my humanity I thought of her as my source, and that's when she didn't show up anymore. God taught me a great lesson.

He uses various channels but He is not bound to any one channel or married to any one method. It is like this. If people went into their kitchen and turned on the water faucet and no water came out, they would not conclude that there was no water left in the world. They would know that there is plenty of water in the reservoir. There was just a problem getting it through their pipes. So sometimes the pipe seems to fail or the water faucet doesn't seem to work correctly; but I have learned that no matter what takes place, there's plenty of water in the reservoir and God meets and supplies all our needs.

One particular day we had a great need in our ministry in Tarpon Springs, Florida. I went to the post office to pick up the mail. Normally, my daughter, Ruthanne does that. In the mail was an overnight envelope. There was no letter, just a check for $100,000. A wonderful doctor and his wife had heard me on television and were moved by the Lord to meet a great need that we had at that time. God came through. Glory be to His Holy Name.

I remember the time when we were seeking to make a payment on our premises in Tarpon Springs. We needed $80,000 but only had $6,000 on hand. It was Monday morning and it was due that day. I said to Maureen that I was going to take a walk at Fred Howard Park Beach nearby, and talk to the Lord about this great need. Just before leaving, I got the urge to go to my rolodex and pull out the telephone number of a man whom I had never had in any of our services. But I had met him on one occasion socially. He was extremely old and I didn't know if he would still be living. I knew he was retired at least partially because of his age. I went to Howard Park, and took out that number. I called his secretary, who put me right through to him. I said "do you know who I am?" He said, "Yes, you are the Irish preacher on television." I said, "Can I come talk to you?" He said, "Yes, certainly come." It took me about an hour to drive there. He told me about his life story, and about his involvement in the war, about building up his business. He then invited me to lunch, and after lunch he started to tell me again about his life story. It was all so wonderful, but I was secretly looking at my watch from time to time and thinking about the $74,000. The hour was getting late. I needed to leave soon because the traffic would be very thick. I needed $74,000!

Well into mid-afternoon I was sitting in his office. He pulled out the drawer of his desk. I didn't know what he was doing as he started to write. It became obvious then that he was writing a check. He folded it and held it up in the air, signaling for me to get up and take this check. He made it clear, that it was a total gift. I have often joked that if you are giving a preacher a check, don't fold it. He wants to see what it is. I opened it, of course, quickly. I was so moved that I went behind the desk and hugged him. He seemed a little awkward at that, as if giving the check was no big deal. I left there immediately and headed home with a check for $74,000. I didn't have time to stop and call anybody, since I didn't have a cell phone at that time. So when I got home Ruthanne, Maureen, LaDonna and Ryan were there. I walked in and I didn't say a word. They were disappointed because, by my face, it seemed to be that nothing had happened. Then they asked me what happened. I went over the whole story of going out to lunch, listening to the man's life story and to the point of the man handing me a check. I said, "he handed me a check." Ruthanne told me that she thought I was going to say for $1,000. And I said, "it's not a loan, but a gift for $74,000." They all, promptly, jumped on top of me and we shouted and glorified God. God had met our needs miraculously. What a God He is.

Let me give you another amazing story. Here is one which doesn't seem so dramatic, but was used by the Lord to show me how much he cares. One particular day, Ruthanne, who looks after the finances, and is the Chief Executive Officer of our ministry, said to me that we needed such and such amount of money that day. She went to the mail box, picked up the mail, and went through it until she got to the last envelope. Before opening it we were only one dollar short after what she had counted up. So it looked like we were home and dry. Obviously, she went ahead and opened the last envelope. I don't remember the person's name but I will always remember that they were from Kenneth City, in the Tampa Bay area of Florida. Their letter went something like this, "I know this isn't much, but I feel greatly exercised of the Lord to send you this cash and to send it immediately. God bless you." In the envelope, with the letter, was included a one dollar bill.

No it doesn't always happen in such an exciting and dramatic way, but God is faithful and He gloriously meets our needs. All we need is faith in the eternal God, who comes through. Sometimes I am tested more than at other times; but God never fails because He gave me that promise long ago when I was still very young, "My God shall supply all your need, according to His riches in glory by Christ Jesus." And should I live until I am 200, I will never be able to fully explain to anybody what that meeting was like with God when He filled me with His word to the point where I knew that promise better than I knew my own name. I knew that no matter what demon fought me, what person would come against me, how big the bills would get from time to time, God would break through to deliver me and the money would be there. I constantly give God all the glory. He has been so faithful right up to this present moment.

BE STILL MY SOUL

Be still, my soul; the Lord is on thy side;
Bear patiently the cross of grief or pain;
Leave to thy God to order and provide;
In every change He faithful will remain.
Be still, my soul; thy best, thy heavenly, Friend
Through thorny ways leads to a joyful end.

Be still, my soul; thy God doth undertake
To guide the future as He has the past.
Thy hope, thy confidence, let nothing shake;
All now mysterious shall be bright at last.
Be still, my soul; the waves and winds still know
His voice who ruled them while He dwelt below.

Be still, my soul, though dearest friends depart
And all is darkened in the vale of tears;
Then shalt thou better know His love, His heart,
Who comes to soothe thy sorrows and thy fears.
Be still, my soul; thy Jesus can repay
From His own fullness all He takes away.

Be still, my soul; the hour is hastening on
When we shall be forever with the Lord,
When disappointment, grief, and fear are gone,
Sorrow forgot, love's purest joys restored.
Be still, my soul; when change and tears are past,
All safe and blessed we shall meet at last.

Catharina von Schlegel
Translated by Jane Borthwick

<small>CHAPTER 8</small>

DUMB REPORTERS

Have you ever met a dumb reporter? I have met only a few of them. Most reporters are bright, intelligent, "on-the-ball" type of people. Of course, as in all professions, there are rogues among them. There are those who want to color or twist the truth. It is either for ratings, to be sensational, or to get recognition, or a raise or promotion of some kind. I have met a few of those "rogues." Let me give you a few examples.

HALE'S "FRIEND"
When American Jim Bakker had his moral failure, it was news not only all over America but around the world. I did not know anything about Jim Bakker or his fall from grace. One newspaper in Ireland, reporting on the scandal, had as its headline, "Hale's friends in drug and sex scandal!" They were not my friends and obviously that kind of journalism is disgusting beyond belief. They did not mind that they lied about me and tried to tie me to a situation of which I knew nothing about and had absolutely nothing to do with. I am not saying that the person who wrote that headline was dumb. I am saying he was a liar and he knew it!

TRICKY QUESTION
On one occasion I called a press-conference in a hotel in down-town Belfast. Quite a lot of reporters showed up. We treated them nicely and served them tea and biscuits. I then answered any and every question I was asked about me, my ministry, and so forth. I answered them "head-on." Finally, I asked if there were any more questions and there were not any. The press-conference had been respectful and seemingly uneventful. As I was announcing the

conclusion, a photographer who was sitting on the very front row raised his hand and said, "Yes, I have a question." I said, "Go ahead." He then complimented me on my suit and asked where I bought it. To me it was no trick question. He was just being nice and complimentary. I had no idea where I got that suit. I wanted to be accurate so I pulled back one side of my coat and looked at the label on the inside pocket. It was made in Florida so I said that. Again the questioner complimented me on the suit and then the press-conference was over. The next day, there was a photograph of me pulling back my jacket with the headline, "Leslie Hale has his suits personally tailored in Florida and flashes the label to prove it."

I am not saying that the writer of that headline was dumb. I am saying, however, that he was dishonest. He gave a totally wrong impression of the press conference and all the questions I had answered.

Solid Gold

Many years ago, when my family still lived in Ireland, we decided to accept an invitation from a TV reporter to conduct an interview in our home. Not too long before that, we had visited America. I had gone into K-Mart and bought a round lamp which was suspended on a chain from the ceiling in the corner of our living room. The whole thing cost a total of thirteen dollars. When the program appeared on TV, they talked about the lamp which was held up by a "solid-gold" chain. I am not saying that TV reporter was dumb. I am saying he was ridiculous and totally dishonest.

Calendar "Confusion"

This one is unbelievable. A TV program was shown about me and my ministry. At one point, a calendar page was shown. The narrator told the people, as the camera zoomed in on a certain date, that it was when I had raised a large offering in the Ulster Hall, Belfast. The camera then zoomed in on another date on the same page. This date was a week or so after the first date, "and this," said the reporter, "is when Leslie Hale bought his home in Florida." The clear message was that I had taken the money from the Ulster Hall offering then flew to Florida and bought a home. However, it was all a great big lie. What the reporter failed to tell his viewers was that I had bought the home in Florida the previous year. By coincidence, it was the same month but it was **the year before!** He also failed to say that I bought that home with a very small down-payment and then got a mortgage like most other people. I am not saying that reporter was dumb. I am saying he was a total liar. I remember my lawyer urging me, at the time, to allow him to sue the TV company. "Then," he said, "you will have all the money you will ever need to build all the buildings you want to."

DRUNK REPORTER

One time a reporter called our church secretary, Joan, in Ireland and asked for "an interview with Leslie." Joan said the reporter was very drunk and that such an interview would not be possible. "Very well," he declared. "I will write the article anyway." Amazing.

On looking back, I am grateful for some great reporters I met. An outstanding one was **David Capper** from Belfast. Another one was **Blair Thompson** from London. They were honest and sought the truth. They investigated everything about our work and ministry and then released a terrific radio program, the theme of which was, "It is not that Leslie Hale has sinned, rather it is about the fact he has been sinned against." Still, I have met a few dumb ones also.

I BARGAINED WITH LIFE FOR A PENNY

I bargained with Life for a penny,
And Life would pay no more,
However I begged at evening
When I counted my scanty store.

For Life is just an employer,
He gives you what you ask,
But once you have set the wages,
Why, you must bear the task.

I worked for a menial's hire,
Only to learn, dismayed
That any wage I had asked of Life,
Life would have willingly paid.

Author Unkown

CHAPTER 9

THE GOOD, THE BAD, AND THE UGLY

The one thing that has totally possessed my life since I was very young is to obey God come what may. Looking back, I am so pleased to be able to say that I have done that very thing. I have obeyed God. Whether He told me to do something that was popular or unpopular, never even came into the reckoning. I love God with all of my heart and my magnificent obsession is to love Him, put Him first, and let nothing come in between us. I have obeyed God.

Right now I can say that I am in the will of God. I could have said that last year, five years ago, ten years ago, and it would all be true. I give God the glory for this and for this passion to always honor Him, love Him, and serve Him fervently. Over the years as I sought to obey God, I had interaction with many people and I witnessed, the good, the bad, and the ugly. I would like to share some thoughts so that maybe others can benefit from some of the things I have been through, whether they seem to be positive or negative.

I thank God for each true friend who has stood by me and this ministry over the many years. I will always be eternally grateful. But others I have found were true judases and traitors. Everyone, especially young Christians and young preachers must know that as sure as there is a Jesus, there is also a Judas. So here are some of my recollections of some of the things I have been through.

First of all I would like to mention Joan Lonsdale, a true friend with an extraordinary sterling character. Joan is a dear friend of my wife Maureen. In fact, she is a wonderful friend of our whole family. She has been involved with our family and ministry about 40 years. She was also our children's baby-sitter. In the church she was the secretary, organist, and general organizer. To this day she is such a close friend. I would say to her, God bless you Joan for the honor and integrity in which you have lived your life. Thank you for your friendship to the Hales and even though we live so far apart these days, our friendship endures. In fact, I know it will endure forever. How wonderful to have a friend like Joan.

Then, of course, on the other hand there is the ugly. I remember one particular person whom I tried to help so much. Looking back on it, I now realize I put far too much time and effort over a period of several years in trying to help this man to make it. I should have realized years ago, and in some ways did, that he would never make it. The problem with him was, and this is a danger that is so prevalent in the church today, that he got it into his head that he was a preacher. He was not a preacher and had absolutely no gift at preaching. In fact, when he would get up on the platform, he would say the silliest and most stupid things. His wife would cringe, not knowing what he would say next. Finally, after investing my time and money over many years in trying to help him, I had an idea. I would send him overseas and take care of all his expenses for a trip where he would simply promote our ministry, sell some of our books, and thereby raise some money for our ministry in Ireland. Well he did go overseas, he did complete that trip, and he did raise money on the books. The problem is I never saw a dime of it. He simply took it and spent it on himself and his family without any conscience or apology to this very day. What a desperate disappointment. It was all rooted in the fact that this man consistently tried to wear a coat that was far too big for him. He should have stayed with visiting people, which he did for quite a while in seeking to bring people either to the Lord or to the ministry. Once it got into his head that he was a preacher, it ruined him forever. I finally got tired of all his lies and pretentions.

Of course I hold absolutely nothing against that man today. I never have and wish him and his family all the best. I would never name him. I do not want to cause him or his family any embarrassment. But what a lesson to learn. Even if you are being pressured, never try to promote a man to be a preacher when he has a zero calling. Don't let him wear a coat that is a thousand times too big for him.

Now let me go back to some of the good things. I remember a young lady who came to our meetings many years ago at Faith Tabernacle in Belfast, and asked us to pray for her husband that he might be saved. Her name was Sally Goudy and her husband was David Goudy. After we had prayed together for quite a period, David came to one of our meetings at Faith Tabernacle and got saved. Time went on and as he was progressing with the Lord, I invited him to become full-time on our staff at Faith Tabernacle. David had worked in a factory and told me personally that he "never in a million years" would have left his job and launched out into the ministry on his own without any guarantee of finances. I was able to pay him his wage and carry the load and try to be a blessing to him. He stayed on our staff, and eventually I bought a dance hall in Moria in Northern Ireland and turned it into a church. I paid the price to raise the money and do what was necessary to get in and made it into a church extension of Faith Tabernacle. I then asked David to become pastor. David and Sally are still pastors of that church today and no doubt do a splendid work for God. What a joy to see people who were products of our ministry, whom we undergirded financially and bought the church for originally do such a great work for the Lord. It is simply wonderful to be able to report something as precious as that.

"LIFE IS SO DIFFERENT SINCE WE BOTH ACCEPTED CHRIST!"
— Personal testimony from Pastors David and Sally Goudy

SALLY

One Saturday night, in the early 70's, another miracle took place in Faith Tabernacle. I was born again - only this time I was born into the family of God. Through no merit of my own, but by realizing that "Ye must be born again," and that "All have sinned and come short of the glory of God," included me, and by accepting Jesus Christ as my Saviour, I had the assurance of sins forgiven and experienced the "Peace of God that passeth all understanding." I could for the first time call God my Father.

If you are unsaved, this may not seem much of a miracle; but just consider that shortly before this, I was bound for eternal hell and now I am bound for Heaven. Almost everyone wants to go to Heaven, but perhaps like me, you had some very preconceived ideas of Christians and Christianity. The remedy for this is a personal experience. Perhaps you are saving your decision for old age. God tells us that now is the day of Salvation (2 Corinthians 6:2). The decision has to be a personal one; no one can choose for you. How true is the little line "it's better felt than telt!"

I was the first one in my family to accept Christ but, praise God, in a short period of time four more members have become Christians. You too could be the starting point in your home.

Before becoming a Christian, I assumed that Christianity was a trial to be endured and a long list of don'ts. I have found that it is pointless to attempt self-reform before salvation. We can leave all things to Christ and come as we are. I can say from experience, "Old things are passed away: behold, all things are become new," (2 Corinthians 5:17) and I now have joy unspeakable and a happiness unkown before.

At Faith Tabernacle, I met Christians of all ages. I would get the spiritual food necessary for growth (2 Peter 2:2) and Christian fellowship as instituted by God's Word (Hebrews 10:25). I never fail to leave blessed and enlightened. To God be the glory.

DAVID

I was brought up in a home where my mother and two sisters were Christians so I heard the Gospel many times, but I had become hardened and indifferent to it. It wasn't until my wife got saved at Faith Tabernacle that I began to take a fresh interest in what this business of "being saved" or "accepting Christ" was all about. After much persuasion by my wife, I went to Faith Tabernacle. Although I felt very much out of place there, I was not treated any differently. People were warm and friendly and they shook my hand as I went in. During each sermon preached by Leslie Hale, I felt that he was speaking directly to me. This made me feel very uncomfortable. I have since learned that this was the Holy Spirit speaking to me and convicting me of my need to accept the Lord Jesus Christ as my Saviour (Hebrews 4:12).

One weekend there was a special visitor at the Tabernacle. This man had given up fame and fortune and had become a Christian. He radiated the love of God. Everyone around was so happy that I decided that I just had to get what these people had. At the end of the service, I accepted Jesus Christ as my personal Saviour. Since that night, I have discovered that true happiness lies in following Christ Jesus. Other things may give a false sense of happiness for a short term, but this joy is everlasting. With Jesus my past is forgiven (Col. 1:14), my future is assured (1 Thess. 4:17), and my present is exciting because every day is different with Christ and getting better as time goes by.

A few months following my conversion, I was one of about twenty people who were baptized in water at a great baptismal service held at the Grove Baths.

The indwelling of the Holy Spirit helps me daily in my new life. Christ is the center of my life now and I know that He cares forever in each department of our being... Soul, mind, and body. Luke 12:7 says, "But even the very hairs of your head are all numbered..." God is up to date in every situation and He wants to help us all if only we will let Him. No wonder the psalmist David wrote, "The Lord is my Shepherd. I shall not want." God is a miracle worker and no problem you have is too big for Him. As Leslie often says, "He is the God of the present —not next week or next year, but NOW." He wants to help you too—do not limit Him.

Jesus Christ is not just a person who lived, was crucified, and died 2,000 years ago. He is the Living Son of God, who is interested in each person individually and who is willing and wanting to save your soul and meet your every need. You too can have Christ as your personal friend today.

I still have a beautiful letter which David Goudy wrote to me. In it he thanked me for taking him out of work and bringing him into the ministry. He said, in the letter, "I would not have a ministry or a church today if it were not for Leslie Hale."

One sad thing happened to David and his church in Moira, Northern Ireland. For a period, the wretched and fleshly "laughing" business penetrated the meetings. At that point I had turned the church over to David and had nothing more to do with it. Still, it hurt to think that a church which I had founded would be caught up in such silly nonsense. David has since recovered and I am delighted.

I want nothing but the best for him. I can sympathize with him very much in that mistake. One time when I was ministering in Helsinki, Finland, a letter arrived from a man in Ireland asking permission to help in our office, so I agreed. What a mistake that was. That man proved to be both a thief and a trouble maker. We all make mistakes but we can all recover.

Then there is Pastor Willie Dick. At the time of writing, Willie and I have been friends for about thirty-nine years. We have been close over the years, and I love him very dearly. He has taken a strong stand for the Lord and honors God in his life. I love to hear him pray and, from time to time, I have called him long distance from America to Ireland, sometimes in the wee hours of the morning, just to get him to pray for the strength of God in my being. His son Stephen works in our office in Florida. He is a wonderful young man and we get along famously. Yes, I thank God for Willie and for his family.

Have you ever been betrayed? I remember many years ago in Northern Ireland when we would ask men to go out on Monday evenings and visit people who had been saved in our Sunday evening service. It seemed a beautiful thing to do to try to establish the new converts in their faith.

Later I found out that rather than helping in the Lord, one of the men we asked to help was actually presenting the "wares" of his business and trying to sell them in his business capacity. I felt so betrayed by this man in that way and other ways. In fact, after stealing names, and phone numbers from our files, he went around spreading lies about us and telling them not to give to our ministry any more. What an ugly situation. It was a terrible Judas spirit.

Then there is John Williamson. Many, years ago I had asked him to go to Toronto, Canada and open an outreach of Faith Tabernacle. John was greatly involved in our work and was blessed so much at Faith Tabernacle. In fact, his wife Christine was saved at Faith Tabernacle, and they learned so much in our meetings, according to their own testimony. When I challenged them about Canada, to their everlasting credit they responded immediately and went and dug out a work from zero. At the time of this writing, they are building a 1,200 seat sanctuary. It is located in Brampton, just immediately outside Toronto. God blessed the two of them through our ministry and now they are going on with the Lord, in love with Him in a wonderful way. What an exciting story.

HE STARTED TO SING AS HE TACKLED THE THING THAT COULDN'T BE DONE AND HE DID IT!

Somebody said that it couldn't be done
But he with a chuckle replied
That "maybe it couldn't," but he would be one
Who wouldn't say so till he tried.
So he buckled right in with the trace of a grin
On his face. If he worried he hid it.
He started to sing as he tackled the thing
That couldn't be done, and he DID it!

Somebody scoffed: "Oh, you'll never do that;
At least no one ever has done it;"
But he took off his coat and he took off his hat
And the first thing we knew he'd begun it.
With a lift of his chin and a bit of a grin,
Without any doubt or quibbling,
He started to sing as he tackled the thing
That couldn't be done, and he DID it.

There are thousands to tell you it cannot be done,
There are thousands to prophesy failure,
There are thousands to point out to us one by one,
The dangers that wait to assail you.
But just buckle in with a bit of a grin,
Just take off your coat and go to it;
Just start in to sing as you tackle the thing
That "cannot be done," and you'll DO it.

(CONTINUED ON PAGE 100)

CHAPTER 10

CASTING OUT
OF DEMONS

In the beginning of my ministry while I was still a young man, I was preaching and praying for the sick in Ireland. I realized that I was being fought furiously from several different quarters. The battles were very fierce. It became increasingly obvious to me that one of the main reasons was because of the great power God had put into my life. As Paul would say, "Whatever you have you received." So there is no self-glory here. God had filled me with His Spirit, His Word, and His power and I knew it. I give him the glory.

One of the areas that this great power was manifested was in the ministry of casting out devils. Now we are very middle of the road, very solid people regarding the foundational truths of the Bible. We are not crazy but we do believe that there are such "things" as demons, as devils, and we are to cast them out forcefully in Jesus' name. We had many dramatic cases of this in Ireland and after one of those cases, I sat down and wrote the following words.

FACE TO FACE WITH DEMONS

I stood in front of the young woman. She was not more than twenty and of slight build. She was one of a number of people who had responded to my invitation to come for prayer. It was after I had preached at Faith Tabernacle in Belfast, Northern Ireland and, as is my custom, I was moving along the line laying hands upon the sick and needy and asking Jesus Christ to make them whole.

But something happened when I was about to pray for this young woman something very different than that which usually happens when prayer is offered. Usually the person cooperates and rejoices over God's blessing but this young woman was different. She talked rationally, and there was no indication whatsoever of what was about to take place.

I raised my right hand to place it upon her forehead. Suddenly, she threw back her head, her eyes leered, her face became cynical, and in a deep masculine voice - completely different from her normal voice - shouted out, *"We have been here too long, we will never leave her!"*

The crowd was shocked and stunned. The young woman swayed back even further. The atmosphere was electrified. Even though we were used to meetings where people rejoice, sing loudly, clap their hands, and so forth, nobody had been expecting this. That anybody would yell at the preacher in the healing line, a place of compassion and helpfulness, was bad enough; but that such a gentle looking young woman should become so possessed as to shout, in a deep masculine voice, was incredible.

People in the line always use the word "I" in the singular to tell of their needs. She used the word "We" in the plural. God quickly showed me that here was a case of demon possession. There are such "things" as demons. They are evil spirits, without a body, who go about seeking whom they can possess. It is important that we live clean Christian lives and thereby keep ourselves free from such devilish spirits. But many do not live right and become possessed.

Before this, God had used me in the casting out of demons. It is clearly taught in the Bible and was an integral part of the ministry of Jesus and the early Apostles.

But it was evident to me that this was a special case. Special in the sense that the young woman was possessed with many demons, and I would need to cast them out forcefully in the mighty name of Jesus. I found so often that if I can keep my hand upon the person's forehead, I have power over the demon forces. If I lose that contact then I must quickly seek to reestablish it. My men who assist me in the healing line know this and they immediately moved in to hold the girl. They used minimum force, of course, but held her so that I could keep my hand upon her forehead and speak to the demons to leave her.

As soon as I touched her, she jerked and twisted violently. I spoke loudly to the Devil to leave her alone! I said that I was coming against him in the name of my Master Jesus and he would have to go.

She slumped to the floor. It took about five strong men to hold her in one place! She took on supernatural strength and poured forth a volume of the most vile curses imaginable. All this was happening in church! Many people got on their knees. Several started to sing songs of victory. Others prayed.

By this time, I was on my knees beside the poor victim of Satan. Her eyes were rolling and she was beside herself. It was terrible to behold. I took my coat off as the perspiration rolled down my face. But Jesus was with me, and He had called me to this ministry of healing the sick and casting out devils. I knew no fear and I knew Satan must go. I was depending entirely upon God to show me what to do, second by second. "I adjure thee - in the name of Jesus Christ the Son of the living God - come out of her!" I commanded. She twisted. It seemed her body was being torn into thousands of pieces; and the most unearthly, indescribable yell I had ever heard poured out from the back of her throat. She screamed, getting louder and louder until it reached a certain point, then it died off and her head would roll to the side. She was utterly exhausted, but the battle was not over. That was only one demon gone, and she had many more demons possessing her. The same thing happened several more times. Each time I would speak, the demons would first swear back at me and then, as they realized they must obey the command given in the authoritative name of Christ, they would leave her with great yells and screams.

God then led me to do an unusual thing. Instead of commanding the next demon to go, I spoke these words, "*Tell me what happened at Calvary?*" An amazing thing happened. Although the young woman's mouth had been hardly closed, with swearing and screaming, her teeth gritted together and her head swung from side to side. "*Tell me,*" I repeated, "*what happened at Calvary?*" I was not, of course, speaking to the young lady. I was speaking to the demons still possessing her, the demons that repeatedly had said, *"We are here too long and we will never leave now."* But now those demons were utterly and completely stunned. They were paralyzed at the very mention of "**Calvary.**" **Thank God for the wonderful victory of Jesus on Mount Calvary!**

She was now strangely quiet, but still twisting and jerking. I felt such sorrow for her. Obviously no one else could help her outside of God. How glad I was that God was on the scene!

The congregation had become quiet also. They were listening for the demons' response. Finally I said, *"All right, I will tell you what happened at Calvary! You were defeated at Calvary!"*

A roar of praise went up from the congregation. More demons came screaming out. We were winning, but still the battle raged. At one stage, she became so quiet and seemingly "**normal**" that, at first glance, it would have seemed that it was all over and she was delivered. But not so. God showed me that this was a trick of the Devil; I was to keep praying until she was fully free and God would witness to me that it was indeed over.

The demons then produced what they thought was their master card. In that horrible rough voice the words came forth, *"You don't know how many of us are still here."* The Bible teaches that a person can be possessed with one or more demons. It was obvious that she had many. Now the question was, *"How many remain?"* No doubt this was calculated to embarrass me in front of the congregation. This would be a score for the Devil, but it wasn't. God, by the gifts of the Holy Ghost, spoke to me in the clearest terms within my soul. *"There are eight of them still there."* I repeated, audibly, what God had said. **"There are eight of you still in there!"** There was again the twisting and jerking, again the groans instead of words, again a great shout of praise from the congregation. There were eight of them still there! Victory was close. Five demons left fairly quickly, one after the other, each with horrible screams.

Finally, God led me to charge the remaining three, as one, to leave. **They did. She was free.** God witnessed to my spirit that it was over. Victory was ours. Victory was hers. An hour and a half had gone by and the congregation was both amazed and thrilled. They had witnessed God's power in action. They had seen a repetition of the Acts of the Apostles. God was performing miracles as He has always done.

The young woman was completely exhausted. She rose to her feet. I instructed a few other Christian girls to take her aside and talk to her and comfort her. She accepted Christ as her personal Savior.

Later, from conversation with her, it was obvious that she had not been aware of half of what had been going on. Now she was happy and she felt free. Something, she declared, had left her life, and Christ had come in instead.

The Bible says that we can cast out devils in His Name. In these last days there is a greater need than ever before for men to seek God's face, hear His voice, receive His power, and set people free.

It's easy to laugh when the battle's fought
And you know that the victory's won;
Yes, easy to laugh when the prize you sought
Is yours when the race is run;
But here's to the man who can laugh when the blast
Of adversity blows; he will conquer at last,
For the hardest man in the world to beat
is the man who can laugh in the face of defeat.

Edgar Guest

Chapter 11

"LET NOT THEN YOUR GOOD BE EVIL SPOKEN OF..."

(Roman 14:16)

Pastor William Dick has been a friend of mine for almost four decades. Over the years, Willie has been most encouraging. We have taken many of the things he has said or sent by e-mail and put them together for this chapter.

MY FRIEND, LESLIE HALE
—By William Dick.

Leslie, I thank God for you. Ireland did not realize what it had and lost. I have known Leslie Hale closely for almost forty years. I have never met a human being so dedicated to God, so humble, so honest, and so gifted as my friend and teacher Leslie Hale. The thing that strikes you the most about Leslie is his total love for God and his total commitment to obey God all the way. I have watched him being attacked ferociously and unjustifiably, but he has never flinched in his obedience to his wonderful Lord.

I particularly think of the time that the Holy Spirit changed Leslie's plans regarding the magnificent vision that God had given to him. Leslie had obeyed God. He had procured land at Glengormley in Northern Ireland. He had built the first beautiful building. When he would preach in it, it would be packed to the doors. Many, many souls came to Christ. Then he started constructing the second building. Things were moving along.

From an obscure boy, he had now become very well known. Thousands sought his prayers for healing and deliverance. Then out of the blue, the Holy Spirit shifted gears. The Lord instructed Leslie to go to America.

We all knew Leslie loved America, but we also knew he would never go to live in America just for selfish reasons. However, when God spoke, he had to obey! It was like something earth-shattering. People rose up against him and fought him. The press had a field day. I observed him closely and he never budged. God had spoken and he must obey! It really was something. He had spent years building a fantastic ministry in Ireland. Literally, thousands had been saved through his ministry. He was Ireland's best known evangelist. Now God was telling him to move to another country and start from scratch - start all over again. He went to America with Maureen and their three young children in total and absolute obedience to God. Leslie never questioned God. I have asked myself this question, "Why?" Why leave an exciting work which had taken years to build? The results were indisputable. Multitudes had been blessed through his ministry. Remember what happened to Paul, "Then Paul and Barnabas waxed bold, and said, It was necessary that the word of God should first have been spoken to you: but seeing **ye put it from you, and judge yourselves unworthy of everlasting life, lo, we turn to the Gentiles**" (Acts 13:46). T.L. Osborn, the world famous evangelist told Leslie at that time, "God is with you. You are in obedience to God."

I also remember what Jesus said, "And whosoever will not receive you, when ye go out of that city, shake off the very dust from your feet for a testimony against them" (Luke 9:5).

I do not know why. Leslie does not know why. However, he totally said "YES" to God. In his first Sunday in America, he had three people in the service. Today it is a thrill to go to Florida and see the vision coming to pass which Leslie talked about all those years ago. The Sanctuary is magnificent and is exactly as Leslie had described it here so long ago. The Antique Bible Museum is one of the finest in the whole world in private hands. The Dining Facility is like a five-star restaurant. Then there is the in-house printing, the TV equipment, the internet, and the raising up of the splendid "Tabernacle-In-The-Wilderness."

In some ways Leslie's story is absolutely fantastic. In other ways it is not a story at all. What do I mean? Let me take the last part first. In these days of "tabloid journalism" people want to read the "juicy" part. They love scandal and negative things in a person's life. In this sense there is no story at all about my friend Leslie Hale. There is no cheating, no lying, no stealing, no drugs, no pornography, no alcohol, no infidelity, nothing illegal, nothing immoral, and nothing unethical. There are no - absolutely no "juicy" parts about this story.

On the other hand, the story of Leslie Hale is a truly remarkable one.

Leslie was born into an extremely shy family in Saint Vincent Street off the Shore Road in Belfast. He had a wonderful childhood with two magnificent parents and two fully supportive sisters. Leslie got saved on his eleventh birthday. Over the next few years the Spirit of God came upon him mightily.

He never wanted to be a preacher but he obeyed God all the way.

He fell in love with Jesus early on and has walked with God ever since. What an anointing is on his life! What a gift of preaching and teaching he possesses.

From a shy boy in St. Vincent Street in Belfast, he now reaches around the world with a pure and powerful ministry of God's Word. To say that God has blessed him is the understatement of the century. By the way, I was there in Belfast when a few men decided to destroy Leslie. I knew these men. They were totally unspiritual and they were complete liars. "Wisdom is justified of her children" (Luke 7:35). I know one man personally who tried to steal Leslie's ministry. When his attempt failed, he lied about Leslie everywhere. In a nut shell, this is one of the things that happened. When Leslie was going to America, this man tried to grab the ministry and all its assets. When Leslie appointed another person as leader, the culprit almost went crazy. He was so full of envy, jealousy, and lies. He set about a diabolical plan to destroy Leslie. Why the news media never investigated this man I will never know. One reporter who did talk to him said, "He is the biggest liar I have ever talked to in thirty years of journalism."

These miserable men have accomplished nothing for God. On the other hand Leslie has moved ahead in total obedience to his Master, the one he loves totally, the Lord Jesus Christ.

I would like to add these few words to my friend, Leslie Hale.

Leslie, thank you for obeying God! Thank you for putting Jesus first regardless of how horribly the devil attacked you. Thank you for being my teacher and thank you for being my faithful friend for all these many years.

I cannot close this chapter without referring to something truly incredible that happened several years ago. It was the way Leslie stood up in Northern Ireland and declared "the Word of the Lord" regarding the country when it looked like the whole of Northern Ireland was hopelessly headed toward a civil war.

It is amazing to me that the press never gave Leslie one ounce of credit for predicting things so correctly. When Leslie told the whole country, "THERE WILL BE NO CIVIL WAR IN IRELAND," it looked crazy with bombs and bullets all around us. When he predicted prosperity for Ulster, it seemed madness. But he was right. It all came to pass exactly as he said.

One last thing, when I look back at the person who tried to steal Leslie's ministry and all its assets and who subsequently slandered Leslie everywhere, it almost makes my blood boil. A person has to be filled with an incredible amount of evil to behave like that in seeking to destroy a wonderful servant of God. The man could not even preach. He has never built a church. How pathetic!

PSALM 15

Within thy tabernacle, Lord,
who shall inhabit still?
Or whom wilt thou receive to dwell
in thy most holy hill?

The man whose life is uncorrupt,
whose works are just and straight,
Whose heart doth think the very truth,
and tongue speaks no deceit;

That to his neighbor doth no ill,
in body, goods, or name;
Nor willingly doth slanders raise,
which might impair the same:
That in his heart regardeth not
malicious wicked men;
But those that love and fear the Lord,
he maketh much of them:

His oath and all his promises
that keepeth faithfully;
Although he make his cov'nant so
that he doth lose thereby:
That putteth not to usury
his money and his coin;
Nor for to hurt the innocent
doth bribe, nor yet purloin.

Whoso doth these things faithfully,
and turneth not therefrom,
Shall never perish in this world,
nor that which is to come.

Scottish Psalter, 1635

CHAPTER 12

A LETTER
TO ULSTER

Northern Ireland is also known as **ULSTER**. It is not strictly nor technically correct but the two names are usually used interchangeably. So I would like to write a letter to Ulster (Northern Ireland).

DEAR ULSTER,

I love you. I was born in your borders. To be exact, I discovered this world on a Thursday (twenty-fifth of May) many years ago. I was born in sixteen St. Vincent Street, off the Shore Road in Belfast, right beside Crusaders Soccer ground. So I grew up supporting the "Crues" and because of my fathers influence, I also loved Glasgow Rangers.

When I was still only twenty, I left my work and entered full-time ministry. I prayed and studied for the first three months and then held my first crusade in a tent in Armagh, Northern Ireland. After that, it was "full-steam" ahead.

Ulster, for years I traveled your roads, sometimes in the wee hours of the morning, as I ministered in town after town all across the province. I preached the pure gospel to you. I told you that **"GOD IS A GOOD GOD."** I told you about **"SAY SO"** - Let the redeemed of the Lord **say so!** I led thousands of you to Jesus. I prayed for multitudes to get healed and many, many testified that they did.

I never cheated anybody.

I never lied to you.

I never hurt a single soul.

God helped me to live a pure, holy life even though I was involved in some powerful, spiritual battles. There never was any infidelity and I was never involved with drugs or alcohol.

I gave myself to you, **Ulster** and there are still many of you living who were either saved, healed, or blessed through my meetings and my total dedication to God and His word. I was fought, ridiculed, and lied about but I never quit. I never even had one single thought about quitting. Never! I was possessed in those days, and still am, with an indescribable passion to obey the God I love so fervently. When I left work to preach full time, **I was in the center of God's will.** When I purchased **"Faith Tabernacle"** on York Road Belfast **I was in the center of God's will.**

Later when I purchased the building next door and enlarged **Faith Tabernacle, I was in the center of God's will.**

When I purchased the **"Tempo"** ballroom in Moria, **I was in the center of God's will.**

When I bought the fields outside Glengormley, **I was in the center of God's will.**

When we raised up **Faith Cathedral (Phase 1), I was in the center of God's will.**

When God diverted my paths to America, **I was in the center of God's will!**

Today, in Florida, I am carrying out the plan God gave us years ago; and **I can tell you for sure I am in the center of God's will.** That's what I have lived for — to obey God.

Ulster, our family gave many years of our lives to be a blessing to you. I am thrilled with the mighty victories wrought during these years. Nobody can deny them.

I am so grateful for the many beautiful e-mails I have received from Ireland, north and south of the border, expressing your love for us and your gratitude for our ministry.

Yes, as I said to Northern Ireland so long ago:

"Ulster will live again!"

"Ulster will love again!"

"Ulster will laugh again!"

GOD MOVES IN
MYSTERIOUS WAYS

God moves in mysterious ways
His wonders to perform;
He plants His footsteps in the sea
And rides upon the storm.

Deep in unfathomable mines
Of never failing skill
He treasures up His bright designs
And works His sovereign will.

Ye fearful saints, fresh courage take;
The clouds ye so much dread
Are big with mercy and shall break
In blessings on your head.

Judge not the Lord by feeble sense,
But trust Him for His grace;
Behind a frowning providence
He hides a smiling face.

His purposes will ripen fast,
Unfolding every hour;
The bud may have a bitter taste,
But sweet will be the flower.

Blind unbelief is sure to err
And scan His work in vain;
God is His own interpreter,
And He will make it plain.

William Cowper

CHAPTER 13

THERE WILL BE NO CIVIL WAR IN IRELAND

In the very late fifties and the early to middle sixties, God let me see what would shortly come upon Ireland. It was not a pretty picture. Mind you, I could not at the time understand it, though I did stand up and share it with people. I told how darkness and sorrow were coming to Belfast and Northern Ireland. I repeatedly used the phrase "blood will flow like a river in Belfast and around this country." I was saying—loud and clear —that violence was at hand.

It could be argued that Ireland has a terrible history of recurring violence. That is true, but I was not being influenced by history and I was certainly not hoping that it would repeat itself. In fact, there was never as much talk about reconciliation and peace as at that time. Yet I knew, I just knew, we were heading for a period of killing and bloodshed. God showed me other things also, including the fact that civil war would not come. I was a very young man when I was declaring these things, but I knew I had heard from heaven. These messages from the Lord were carried in our magazine reaching multiplied thousands of people throughout the country. On a number of occasions I also bought space in the country's largest newspaper and the messages were carried on half-page spreads.

Here are some of the words I wrote under the heading, "There will be no civil war in Ireland."

(FOLLOWING ARTICLE WAS WRITTEN IN THE SIXTIES)

"There will be NO Civil War in Ireland. That is a fact. Some years ago, God let me see the situation as it is upon Ulster today. I do not mean I saw every detail. I did, however, see enough to tell many people about it. I told them that "blood would flow in the streets" and the most evil things imaginable were about to take place.

All too terribly, it has all come to pass. There was something else. I was made to understand that we would come to the very brink of Civil War, but that Civil War would not come!

What will come then?

If Civil War does not come to Ulster, what will then take place? I am left in no doubt as to what will happen in the days that lie ahead.

ULSTER WILL PROSPER AS NEVER BEFORE IN ITS HISTORY.

I am well aware, of course, of all the negative talk. "Ulster is finished" has fallen from ten thousand lips. Ulster, however, is not finished. Ulster will prosper unbelievably. I am not saying that I know the political or military details of what is going to happen. I am not a politician and have utterly no desire to ever be one.

I am speaking as a man who has heard from heaven. I do not know the details. Many aspects of the whole question I cannot answer. I can say, however, that Civil War will not come, but prosperity will.

New jobs, new growth, and new business expansion will all take place. Things will be better in the future for the ordinary man and woman in Ulster - regardless of religious or political background - than ever it was in the past.

Tourism will increase remarkably. More money will be available and prosperity will be across the land.

PEACE AND NORMALITY WILL RETURN.

Many at this stage think this impossible. This is not only "not impossible," but it is most assuredly going to happen. At this moment it is hard to think of Ulster without bombs, bullets, murders, troubles, intimidation, fear, and all the other "fall-out" of this tragic situation.

Many have said, "It will never end." Yes, it will end. Again, I do not know the details, but God has certainly told me that peace and normality will be ours - right across the Province.

I do not mean that Ulster will suddenly become Heaven. We will always have trouble, crime, sin, and so forth. There will always be the wrong doers. Ulster is no different and will be no different to any other country in this respect. But as far as the present state of unrest is concerned - the bombings, murders, shootings, etc. will cease. Peace will return. It will return in such a way that people will feel ordinary again. We shall be able to go out shopping, to church, to business, to pleasure, feeling as secure and as ordinary and as peaceful as any person living in an "ordinary" situation.

I know these things are terrible - for everybody - as they are now. Things will change, however; God has told me! Peace and normality, thankfully, will be ours.

Thirdly, Ulster will become one of the world's foremost countries for the spreading of the Gospel of Jesus Christ.

Ulster has always had plenty of religion. I am not now talking of mere "religion" as such. I am talking about an evangelistic, missionary thrust from these shores to the ends of the earth! We will send out more missionaries than ever before. More Gospel literature and more means of communicating the Gospel will be used than can ever be imagined at this time. Records, tapes, television, radio, etc. will all be employed to send the good news of Christ to millions around the globe.

As you see, I am not talking about a few little religious "happenings." I am literally talking about Ulster becoming world famous as the land from which the Gospel is "beamed" to the entire earth.

Ulster, indeed, is on the verge of revival! It is always darkest just before the dawn. Why, the very stars don't shine until it's dark enough. What have these terrible troubles taught us? That we need God. Not the God of history and religion, but the God of power, of understanding, and love. We need to know the God who does things, who sets people free, who brings happiness to our lives and homes, who heals our bodies and minds, and who prospers us in our daily affairs. That's the kind of God we need to know about - and the kind of God we are going to have.

Finally, I say this. God is still on the throne of Heaven and the universe. We, as mere mortals, do not understand all the whys and wherefores. What we have to do is to have faith, to believe, to praise the Lord for the victory and to thank Him for meeting all our needs.

No, Civil War will not come, but revival, prosperity, and peace will. That is for sure.

I do not believe that Ulster will have Civil War. It seems that the citizens of Northern Ireland have come to the brink of it several times and in some ways have actually lived on the brink, but Civil War has not come and I do not believe it will. I have no political reasons for saying that. I have no military philosophy either. I say it because God told me so. The devil has made Ulster famous. God will take advantage of that fame and the world will talk about the wonderful works of God in this place.

Here are the words of a large advertisement which I ran in the country's largest newspaper, *The Belfast Telegraph*, at that time.

WHAT IS GOING TO HAPPEN TO IRELAND NOW?

"Everybody wants to know what is to become of Northern Ireland, or even in a larger context, what is to become of Ireland?

Two great powers have their eyes on Ireland, both, of course, for different reasons. I am not speaking of the United States of America and Russia. I am speaking about God and the devil.

The devil wants Ireland! That may appear very primitive language, but it is telling the fact in as few words as possible.

So, too, does God want Ireland.

Both these great "super-powers" want to use Ireland for their own ends. Ireland is a very strategic country, for two reasons:

(1) Its geographical position.

(2) Its religious heritage.

The devil wants it because of its geographical position. God wants it because of its religious heritage.

The devil can use Ireland's position. God can use Ireland's heritage.

At the moment the battle rages. What is going to happen?

God is going to win.

Ireland is quite a large island separated from the British mainland only by a very short strip of water. For instance, to fly to the British mainland cities from Belfast is only like a hop: thirty minutes to Glasgow, fifty minutes to London. A ship can cross from Ireland to Scotland in ninety minutes at one point. Ireland is also the most westerly country before coming to America. As a base, its strategic value is incalculable. The great Winston Churchill paid tribute to this fact and the great help that Northern Ireland was to the rest of Britain during the last war.

What an island for the devil to have!

What a base for the forces of evil to control!

With America away to one side and Britain a step on the other, wouldn't Satan love to stamp out God's work and God's name in Ireland and use it as an atheistic launching-pad to cause sorrow all over Britain, Europe, and further afield? So the devil is after Ireland to use it for his own evil ends.

God is also after Ireland because of its religious heritage. In this country - both North and South - people have been taught to fear God. There is a background of religion, and there are churches everywhere. God's hand is upon Ireland, and it will be used to send the Gospel all over the world in the days to come. When God gets through to the Irish people, through a great Holy Spirit revival, He will convert that religious heritage into a dynamic relationship with Himself. When that happens, multitudes of Irish people - again North and South of the border - will be on fire for God and not only will we have great blessing here; but we will send out the Gospel of power to the ends of the earth.

The devil wants to hurt Ireland and then use it as a launching-pad to hurt others. God wants to bless Ireland and then use it as a launching-pad to bless others. God will win.

The troubles have truly been terrible, just as surely they are passing. Northern Ireland will laugh again!"

IF

If you can keep your head when all about you
Are losing theirs and blaming it on you;
If you can trust yourself when all men doubt you,
But make allowance for their doubting too;
If you can wait and not be tired by waiting,
Or, being lied about, don't deal in lies,
Or, being hated, don't give way to hating,
And yet don't look too good, nor talk too wise;

If you can dream - and not make dreams your master;
If you can think - and not make thoughts your aim;
If you can meet with triumph and disaster
And treat those two imposters just the same;
If you can bear to hear the truth you've spoken
Twisted by knaves to make a trap for fools,
Or watch the things you gave your life to broken,
And stoop and build 'em up with worn-out tools;

If you can talk with crowds and keep your virtue,
Or walk with kings - nor lose the common touch;
If neither foes nor loving friends can hurt you;
If all men count with you, but none too much;
If you can fill the unforgiving minute
With sixty seconds' worth of distance run -
Yours is the Earth and everything that's in it,
And - which is more - you'll be a Man my son!

Rudyard Kipling

CHAPTER 14

THROWN OUT OF EVERY PUB IN BELFAST
(An Amazing Story)

The Leslie Hale Ministry airs a one hour telecast each week in the United States. It is shown in the Tampa Bay area at 9pm on Saturdays—prime time. A telephone number comes on the screen so that viewers can call in with prayer requests and so forth.

The telephones are answered by a group of dedicated "telephone prayer partners." On a recent Saturday evening, a remarkable exchange took place between a viewer and a telephone partner.

It went like this:

CALLER: (In a broad Belfast accent) "Is this the Leslie Hale show?"

PRAYER PARTNER: "Yes, can I help you?"

CALLER: "Ah, cert'ny." *(yes, certainly)*

PRAYER PARTNER: "How can I help you?"

CALLER: "I just want to inform you about yer man."

PRAYER PARTNER: "You mean Leslie Hale?"

CALLER: "Yip."

PRAYER PARTNER: "Do you know him?"

CALLER: "I know him very well - very pers'ly." *(personally)*

PRAYER PARTNER: "What do you know?"

CALLER: "I'm from Belfast and I know him well. I just want you to know the facts."

PRAYER PARTNER: "What facts?"

CALLER: "About yer man."

PRAYER PARTNER: "What about him?"

CALLER: "He's been thrown outa every pub in Belfast!"

What you just read actually happened and it gave rise to the title of this chapter. The caller of course was not laughing. He was telling "the honest truth." It makes no difference that Leslie has never had even one alcoholic drink in his entire life.

The Belfast visitor to Tampa had "the facts" and he was determined to share them with one and all.

When Leslie heard the story, he roared with laughter. Yet it does bring up a serious point. Why would such a man lie through his teeth like that? One can only imagine the number of people on both sides of the Atlantic who have now been informed about Leslie's exits from every pub in the city. Actually it is very sad. Most people from other countries, upon seeing one of their fellow country men on television overseas, would probably say something complimentary. Not so with our gallant Belfast man.

What you are about to read in this chapter will probably amaze you. Your first thought will probably be - "Why didn't Leslie write these words years ago?"

Leslie is a man of God anointed by the Holy Ghost and has brought joy and help to multitudes. He is a credit to Northern Ireland and a shining example of how a true Christian can stand fast in the face of every lie and attack imaginable. Some people will of course continue in their lies about Leslie Hale, but today they are a very small and very insignificant number. They have been disgraced and discredited, and their ridiculous charges have collapsed under their own weight. Just think of this. Maybe Leslie can be a tremendous blessing to you as he has been to so many others. Read this book with an open mind. Be fair. Maybe Satan, through foolish agents, has sought to distance you from Leslie so that you would not receive the blessing which you otherwise would have through his ministry. Listen to him preach. He has a tremendous talent from God. Listen to his CD's and DVD's. Read his literature. You'll be glad you did. You'll get a better understanding of God and faith will be stirred in your heart.

Listen To Leslie

Here is an amazing story. Some years ago I was standing, looking in through the shop window of a Christian bookstore.

After several moments, I became aware of a figure standing beside me. The person shuffled a little closer and began to speak. When I looked, I saw that the man had the traditional Irish flat cap and scarf tied about his neck.

His first comment was a question. He asked me if I knew Leslie Hale. I kid you not, that was his first question. I simply asked him if he knew Leslie Hale. "Do I know him," he said, "I most certainly do. I know him exceptionally well. I've known him for several years, and I can tell you some things about him. First of all, he knows nothing about the Bible." The man then proceeded to tell me about his personal friendship with Leslie Hale and how bad a man he was. Finally he told me that I should take heed of his warnings and never, ever have anything to do with "that man." In a few minutes he shuffled out of my life again. I have never seen him since then and, of course, I never told him to whom he was speaking.

This is a true story. In some ways it is funny, and in some ways it is sad. Is there no way to get rid of the small-mindedness that has beset Northern Ireland? In some ways I see healthy signs that there may be changes coming along this line; but there is still too much bigotry and spite, based on hearsay or outright lies.

The other story is also true, but it can only be called "weird" - weird in every sense of the word. It took place much more recently and, while I cannot give the full details, I can tell you that there was a phone call between a person in Northern Ireland, from the Country Antrim area, with a person overseas. The conversation was about me. What the person in County Antrim never knew of course, was that I was privy to what was going on.

Of course, the County Antrim man had nothing good to say. If he had merely stated that he disagreed with me theologically or philosophically, that would have been fair enough, but boy, did he ever get into a roll! Words were flying out of his mouth at an incredible rate, telling one absurdity after another with utterly no basis in fact whatsoever. He told of a supposed time and occasion when he and his wife went to one of our meetings and I was able, so he said, with some magical power, to announce how much money his wife had in her purse. I know by this time you're laughing, but hold on, there's more to come.

There never was a feeling from our County Antrim hero that since he was speaking to a total stranger, whose credibility he had never checked out, that maybe he should hold fire or go easy on the lies or maybe even stand up for Leslie, seeing that at least he and Leslie are both men from Northern Ireland - a kind of a camaraderie spirit you know. Oh no, there was nothing like that. He was absolutely on fire in his hatred and bitterness.

Needless to say, I don't know the man at all, and his stories were so absurd that they are not worth repeating. The tragedy is that he claims, evidently, to be a Christian even though his gossip, lies, hatred, and spite for a man that he doesn't even remotely know are all condemned by God's Word. He probably would have passed out had he known that I was privy to all that he said; but it did make me realize, with sadness, the kind of craziness that I am dealing with.

How sad when so called "Christians" in Northern Ireland can give themselves totally to lies and perversion, seemingly all without even a twinge of conscience. While listening to the Country Antrim man's asinine comments, I realized that I was not dealing with a Christian but with a religious pervert and a mental midget.

In spite of everything, God's call is upon my life. I love Him with all of my heart, and I'm doing my best to obey Him each step of the way. God bless you as you walk with God and find out how wonderful a Saviour He is.

It is a fantastic experience to walk and talk with God and live in obedience to Him and His calling. He has been so good to me and my family. I am sharing my story, at this time, under His direct instruction.

"I thought it good to shew the signs and wonders that the high God hath wrought toward me. How great are His signs! and how mighty are His wonders! His kingdom is an everlasting kingdom, and His dominion is from generation to generation" (Daniel 4:2-3).

QUESTIONS & ANSWERS WITH LESLIE FROM A RECENT INTERVIEW

Q: When did you accept Christ?

A: I was born again on my eleventh birthday. That means that every time the 25th of May comes around, I have two birthdays—my natural and my spiritual. Even before I accepted Christ, I was deeply moved by the things of God. I remember, for example, lying in the back room of our little house as a boy, with tears running down my cheeks, singing these words, as I looked up to heaven,

"Take my life and let it be,
Consecrated Lord to Thee.
Take my moments and my days,
Let them flow in ceaseless praise."

Q: Where did you work before entering the ministry?

A: Before I became a full time preacher, I only had two jobs. One was working for a lawyer at a company called J.C. Taylor (now known as Fisher&Fisher). In fact, J. C. Taylor is our ministries' lawyers to this day. Then I worked for over four years at the Inglis Biscuit and Cake Bakery at Connswater on the east side of Belfast.

Q: When did you commence full time ministry?

A: I left my employment at the Inglis Biscuit and Cake Bakery on the May 6, 1960, which means I have been in full-time ministry for well over forty years at this point.

Q: Have you traveled extensively since then?

A: Yes, I have traveled to many countries in different continents. I have preached, of course, all over Northern Ireland and as far away as South Africa.

Q: Where did you have your first headquarters building?

A: The first headquarters building that I had was located on York Road in Belfast. Later on we also turned part of the same building into a church, where over the years, thousands of people got saved, healed, or filled with the Holy Spirit. Multitudes look back to that building on York Road as a place of Divine destiny in their lives.

Q: Whom did you buy that building from?

A: From a very fine Belfast businessman called Mr. John Crowe. We took possession of that building in 1962. Then a number of years later, bought the adjoining building from the Northern Bank.

Q: Are you a pastor?

A: I was a traveling Evangelist for many years. Today I am a Pastor / Domata. My primary ministry is to teach God's Word.

Q: How long ago was it since you first visited America.

A: I first visited America in November 1963. As a matter of fact, I was actually in America when President Kennedy was assassinated. I then traveled to and from America many times over the ensuing years.

Q: When did you move to America?

A: I moved to America in 1981, but I continued to travel back and forth between America and Northern Ireland very regularly for several years.

Q: Why did you move at all to the USA?

A: There is no other answer except the most wonderful one, which is simply that I did it in obedience to the Holy Spirit. Nothing else matters in my life like obeying God, and I am in His will today as I was in His will back then when I made the move.

I do remember, just before leaving Northern Ireland in 1981, that the world famous evangelist, T.L. Osborn, told me that he knew that I was in God's will. I remember also, another very well-known preacher called Norvel Hayes, telling me at that time, "Leslie, many will not understand this move, but God has shown me that you are exactly in His will." As I said before, I was in His will then and I am in His will today.

Q: Why Florida?

A: People who do not know the facts have come up with all kinds of answers as to why I moved to Florida. Some said it's because of the sunshine; some said it's because I wanted to live near Disney Word. Well, the sunshine is nice and Disney World is wonderful, but the only reason I'm in Florida is because of the guidance of the Holy Spirit. If God had guided me to one of the jungles of Africa, I would have gone just as instantaneously.

Q: Did your whole family go with you?

A: Of course. Maureen and my three children, Ruthanne, Leslie and LaDonna Raquel, all went together as a family unit. We are a very close family who love each other fervently. It was a joy to be together then and it's a joy to continue to be together today.

Q: What are you presently doing in America?

A: I am carrying out the vision God gave me years ago.

Q: It was widely reported that several years ago when you went to America at the beginning, you never told your congregation. Is that true?

A: That story was told by a man who lost his position within our ministry. Of course, it is totally absurd and untrue. I got up and told the congregation what I was doing; that I was going to America to internationalize our work.

Q: How much money did you take with you to America in 1981?

A: A few hundred dollars, most of which came from a paid-up policy that my mother had paid for sixteen years on our daughter Ruthanne. We had only money for food for a few weeks, but we were happy to be going in God's will.

Q: Leslie, this is amazing. Was it not rumored that you took thousands from the ministry in Ireland and bought property in Florida?

A: You just put your finger on the problem when you used the word "rumored." Again, these stories were told by those who had an axe to grind and who backslid and were not flowing in the Holy Spirit. They told the most outrageous lies. I say again, of course we did not take "thousands." I have already answered how much we did take in the last question, and so I can lay to rest once and for all this absurd charge of us taking a large amount of money from the ministry.

As a matter of fact, we took nothing from the ministry. When I went to America, we paid for the church with $100 down. We bought the house with a small down-payment and got a mortgage just like everybody else - and by the way, we already had that house a year before. I had been traveling to America a lot, and the Lord led me to get that house both as a base for when I was in America and also for vacations. In fact, a lot of British people have done a similar thing, and got homes in Florida.

At that time, I had no intention of actually staying in America, but a year later when the Lord did lead us there, then we already had the house.

I also need to point out something here which was typical of the horrendous attacks upon me and my family at the time. A TV program was made about me wherein they pointed out that we had received a large offering in Ireland, I believe it was in the Ulster Hall, and then they said in the same month I bought the house in Florida. Of course, they were making it look like I took the money from the Ulster Hall, went to Florida and paid cash for the house. They didn't have the honesty to say that while it was coincidentally the same month, I actually had the house from the previous year. Nothing was bought in cash, except, of course, a small down-payment. I remind you again, that was the previous year.

The kind of press that we received on the word of people who were not even in touch with God or with the facts was absolutely incredible. But then again, the Bible does teach that we are going to be persecuted for righteousness' sake, and so we praise the Lord in spite of the attacks.

Q: Why do you think these lies were told about you?
A: Well, there are a number of reasons for that. The Bible itself asks the question: "Why do the heathen rage, and the people imagine a vain thing?" Then the Bible gives the answer; they are gathered together "against the Lord, and against His Christ." I could put that

into more modern English, and here's exactly what it means: "Why do those who are out of touch with God rage and get mad with those who are in touch with God, and who are anointed by the Holy Ghost? It is because they are gathered together against the Lord and against His anointed" (Psalm 2:1).

This will be hard for some people to understand, but God's anointing rests upon my life. His power came into my life many years ago, not only to preach the Gospel, but also to help bring healing to the sick and to cast out devils. As a result of that anointing in my life, a great opposition has been stirred up against me. I have seen people go out of their way to tell the most incredible lies.

I had one man say that he would "blacken me wherever he would go." Another man said that it was his life's ambition to destroy Leslie Hale. Still a third man said these exact words to me sitting in a car, "My mission in life is to destroy your mission in life." I never did one thing wrong to any of those three people. As a matter of fact, I went out of my way for a number of years to try to be a blessing to them, but they wouldn't go through with God. They backslid, got filled with satanic power, and rose up against me and my ministry. Of course, we must understand when we are called of God and His anointing is upon us, that we are foreigners in this world. We are just pilgrims passing through. We are not in some popularity contest. Jesus said, "If the world hate you, ye know that it hated me before it hated you" (John 15:18). I remind you again that the Bible does says, "Blessed are ye, when men shall revile you, and persecute you, and shall say all manner of evil against you falsely, for My sake. Rejoice, and be exceedingly glad; for great is your reward in heaven..." (Matthew 5:11-12).

And so, the question is, why were these lies told against me? Because God is with us in a powerful way, and we can expect fierce opposition. Jesus warned us of this. It happened to Him. It happened to Paul. It happened to Joseph. It happened to anybody throughout church history who obeyed God, and it happens today to those who continue to obey God.

I am not in this ministry for just a little entertainment or a little politics. I wage war against satanic powers, and the devil raises up people to fight me. I understand it, and I can handle it. I must add one other point: One of the three people who I have just referred to, while he was seeking to destroy me, was aware of the fact that I knew about his own moral failure. I made it clear that if he lied about me, I would have to tell the truth about him.

Q: Why did you not try to defend yourself?

A: The answer is, the news media loves something juicy about a well-known person, especially a well-known preacher, and they simply were not interested in my side of the story. They would cut out important things which I would say in my defense when they would give the reports.

I remember one reporter who used to call our office regularly, and would be drunk. I remember another reporter calling from a so-called "prestigious" newspaper in London, and he told my wife that they already had written the conclusion of the story. They had made judgments about me and knew none of the facts, but yet wanted to talk to me so that they could get some background information. That may be hard to believe, but that's exactly what happened. I could give you many such instances.

So why did I not try to defend myself? Well, what way? I could not purchase time on radio or television because they would not give me such time. Besides, at that point the Lord showed me something that gave me great strength and comfort, and I want to relay it at this time. I am not going to say that this was a vision, but it was like a picture in front of my eyes that I could see clearly. It was of a man walking down a road dressed up in a business suit; he had a briefcase and was striding forward to accomplish his work. As he was walking down the road, there was another man in a mud-pit on the side of the road who started throwing mud at him on the way by. The temptation, of course, was for the man in the clean suit, who was going to do wonderful things, to get so mad that he would jump into the pit and start to fight with the person who was attacking him.

As the Lord showed me this picture, He gave me these following thoughts: He said, "Son, the reason why they are throwing mud at you is not merely to smear your good name and the wonderful, honorable name of the Hale family. The primary reason is so that Satan will stop you from accomplishing your task, so whatever you do, do not jump into the pit."

And then, another thing that the Lord showed me was this; He said, "If you do jump into the pit and start to fight, it will end up pretty soon that nobody will be able to tell the good guy from the bad guy. Both of you will be filled with mud." Further more, the Lord showed me that the people who live in the mud-pit are better at throwing mud than I am; and so the best thing for me to do, generally speaking, would be to march on even though there may come a day, as it has happened now, when I could put at least some of the record straight.

But then, what about the mud? Well, God showed me what to do about that. He said, "If you start to try to wipe it off, you will only spread it." He said, "Just keep walking on and eventually it will dry up and drop off." And you know, that is exactly what has happened. Thousands of people love me and my family and my ministry. Multitudes have been helped through us, and they have realized long ago that the wild lies of these God-haters are so absurd that they have now fallen under their own weight.

Q: Have you ever been the victim of thieves?

A: Have I ever! We have had money and goods stolen. We have been the victims of many crimes, perverse stories, smears, and threats. In fact, I remember once standing in Heathrow Airport in London, when a man walked up to me and handed me a note. I read it and it was a threatening letter. There are crazy people in this world!

Regarding being the victim of thieves, I would say that what the devil and his cronies have sought to do mostly is to take away my good name and credibility. I was raised to believe that, "It is a sin to tell a lie," and that a man's word is his bond. I was raised to believe strictly in honesty and integrity, and I always have. And so I can see how the enemy has wanted to hurt us by lying about our integrity. However, God knows the truth and while men may seek to trash our reputation, God knows our character.

Here is a very important observation on this point. I have ministered in Northern Ireland for over thirty years, most of the time while living in Ireland full-time. If we had been involved in anything immoral or illegal, don't you think my enemies would have trailed those out long ago instead of resorting to the smoke-screens that they produce and the innuendos and suggestions which long ago have been proven to be groundless?

I say again, just think about that point. If there really was something wrong, don't you think it would have come out after over thirty years - particularly when we have been attacked by such vicious, hate-filled people?

To answer your question, yes, I have had many things stolen from me; but I still have the Lord, my family, my friends, God's blessing upon my life, and perhaps above all, God's approval and anointing upon my life. What more can a man ask for?

Sometimes we have to "lose" our lives in order to find them again and to find them unto life eternal. I suppose I have been the victim of thieves in various ways over the years; but I have no feelings of loss whatsoever, because in the midst of it all, I have gained Christ and that's all that matters.

Q: Leslie, this is a personal question but here it is. Have you ever had a moral failure?
A: No, never.

Q: Are there any "skeletons in the closet?"
A: No, there is no lying, no stealing, no infidelity, no drugs, no alcohol, and no pornography. God has helped me to live a holy life and to walk daily with Him.

Q: Do you believe God still speaks to men today?
A: Why of course. According to Hebrews 13:8, Jesus Christ is the same yesterday, and today, and forever. God speaks in various ways. He speaks through His Word. He speaks through His Holy Spirit. Sometimes He speaks though others to an individual's heart.

Q: Has God ever spoken to you?

A: Yes. I have heard God's voice on several occasions. I have never heard His voice audibly but I have certainly heard His voice inside my being, giving me specific instructions to do certain things. The Bible says, "My sheep hear my voice, and I know them, and they follow me" (John 10:27). Over the years I have gotten to know His voice. Let me just give you an illustration: If a number of ladies were in one room and I was in another and several called out my name, I would immediately know which one was the voice of my wife, because I know her. Likewise, although I realize there are many voices in this world, a sign of Christian maturity is that you can get to know God's voice.

Q: Tell us about soul-wining. How many souls have you won to the Lord?

A: I have no idea. However, we are talking about thousands of people. Maureen and I poured our lives into Ireland and into other places before coming to America, and nobody can ever deny that God blessed our ministry mightily. I can go back to anywhere I have ever been, knowing that I coveted no man's gold or silver or apparel. His anointing rests powerfully on my life, and I give Him all the glory. He, by His grace, has enabled me to live a godly life all these years.

Q: Why do you think that you have encountered such financial battles?

A: Well, that is in some ways a strange question. Some people want to know the answer to that question, and at the same time others accuse me of being a billionaire. There is quite a dichotomy here. People do not seem to be able to make up their mind on whether I have no money, or whether I have a fortune. Of course, both extreme positions are obviously wrong.

You ask why have I had such financial battles. I think most everybody experiences financial battles, particularly in God's work. In my particular instance, I fought some incredible things. After I went to America I had some people - one individual in particular - who set off on one of the most vicious lying campaigns imaginable by personally visiting home after home of some of my best supporters and partners and lying to them, in order that not only would they stop giving, but that His own predictions of our work coming to a halt would be fulfilled.

Few preachers in Northern Ireland have ever had to face such a thing, and remember, this was happening when I was thousands of miles away in another country. However, time and evidence have proved not only that he and others lied, but that their plot failed.

Q: Here is an unusual question. A reporter says that he was in a meeting of several reporters where they had been informed by one of your enemies that you had taken finances from the ministry over a period of years and bought several rental properties in Southern Ireland, which became the source of your own personal money - the rental money from Southern Ireland. Could you comment on that?

A: Sometimes when a person is lying about another person, they will take even a tiny part of truth, twist it out of all recognition, and make it, into a lie. However, these things which have been told about me, and certainly this present one, have not got even the remotest inkling of truth whatsoever. They are so absurd and so ridiculous.

There are no rental properties. There never were any rental properties. It is a vain imagination of an evil, hate-filled man, and what a tragedy to see somebody backslide so far and sin against their soul by inventing such garbage. By the way, I have heard about that report myself, for one of the reporters told me about it also. I can categorically tell you, it is 100% false in every shape and form and always was.

Q: We understand that you and your wife are owners of a number of hotels or motels in Florida.

A: These things get more absurd all the time. No wonder for years I refused to answer them. They do not deserve an answer. They are below any kind of dignity whatsoever but because of this particular interview, let me give the answer. The answer is a categoric no.

Q: Isn't it true that you lost a lot of money in a libel case in Northern Ireland?

A: No it is not. I have never been in a libel court in my life and therefore never lost a dime.

Q: Sometime back the *Sunday World* newspaper, printed in Dublin, had a headline which said, "Hale's Friends in Sex and Drug Scandal." Could you please elaborate on that?

A: This is still another example of a most vicious type of journalism. It is also, of course, "yellow journalism." The article was about Jim Bakker and Jimmy Swaggart, with whom I do not have, and I have never had, any connection whatsoever in any way, shape, or form. However, the paper felt, no doubt, that they could sell more copies and get more publicity by bringing my name into the article. The article itself hardly referred to me, but the banner headlines tied me to a sex and drug scandal which I have absolutely nothing to do with and never had anything to do with in any way whatsoever.

Q: Leslie, you have told the story about the man sitting in a car with you outside Carrickfergus castle in Country Antrim, Northern Ireland and the horrible words he said to you. How do you feel about that man today?

A: I suppose the word "pity" is the main feeling I have. As you know, he said, "My mission in life is to destroy your mission in life." That goes back almost 40 years and he has stayed true to his mission. The crazy thing is how I tried to help him - financially as well as spiritually. Of course, my respect for him is totally zero. It takes an amazing amount of hatred, jealousy, and envy to keep up a "hate" campaign for so long. All that he has said over the years are total lies. If he had had something truthful about me that was bad, he would have told the world. Yes, pity. He could have been filled with the Holy Spirit instead of being controlled by Satan. I have learned that as sure as there is a Jesus, just as sure there is a Judas.

Q: It has been said that your ministry, on one occasion, was reported to the police. Is that true?

A: This would be a joke of the century if it wasn't so serious. Before I answer it, let me say this; I believe that the police in Northern Ireland should prosecute a person who wastes their time in order to fulfil a personal vendetta. Of course it was an absurdity.

The police officers told us that if somebody reported that we even broke a window, they would have to investigate it. As you know, the police did not pursue the case and it was dropped years ago. I ought to be known as the man falsely accused. I say, anybody who wastes the time of the police in Northern Ireland, realizing how stretched they are with terrorism, not only ought to be ashamed of himself, but he himself ought to be prosecuted, whoever he was.

Q: How did you feel about the BBC radio people arriving in Florida to check out your ministry there? The BBC, I understand, sent top investigative reporters, one from Belfast and one from London?

A: This happened some years ago. I did not know they were coming; but the good thing was that they sent two men who were the epitome of what reporters ought to be, professional and honest in every sense of the word. One was David Capper from Belfast, and the other was Blair Thompson from London. Although I did not know they were coming, I met with them and, they took six hours of recordings. This was narrowed down, if my memory serves me right, to a program approximately one hour long and was put out by the BBC both at home and abroad.

Those two investigative reporters found absolutely nothing. As a matter of fact, David Capper summed up his report with this classic statement; "Leslie Hale is the man who has been more sinned against than sinned." I think people ought to remember that. In no way am I claiming perfection. But when we are talking about morality or evil, then Mr. Capper and Mr. Thompson know that I have been charged falsely and to their credit, they put out a fair program.

Q: It has been stated Leslie, with absolute authority, that when you bought your home several years ago on the Antrim Road in Belfast, it cost £120,000. Now, we know that £120,000 is a lot of money, but obviously back then it was a fortune. Would you comment on that?

A: This is another total, absurd lie. When I bought my house off the Antrim Road from my dear friend, Mr. Sid Scott, it cost precisely £11,250. Any reporter could have checked the public records years ago and found out the truth of that statement. That is what it cost. This figure of £120,000 is an absurdity.

Q: You said your house was off the Antrim Road. I understood that your house was a large one on the Antrim Road, with a heated driveway?

A: I have never owned a house on the Antrim Road. That house with the heated driveway was owned by my friend, Mr. Sid Scott. Incidentally I should tell you that Sid told me of an instance where a reporter from Dublin knocked on his front door to interview Leslie Hale. When Sid told him nicely that Leslie did not live there, the reporter refused to accept it. He told Sid that he had no need to cover up because he had the inside information that Leslie Hale did live there. After a bit, Sid got exasperated and told him to leave, but we still don't think that the reporter was ever convinced.

This makes me think of another little story. A reporter once pressed upon me to let him into my house off the Antrim Road, which cost £11,250. He said he wanted to do a fair report, but he said it appeared that we had a very expensive lamp hanging on "a solid gold chain from the ceiling." As a matter of fact, I had bought the lamp and the chain in a store called K-Mart in America, for only $13.

Q: Thousands of people have been told that you own or did own one or two and maybe three Rolls Royces at one time or another?

A: Boy oh boy! The stories get more absurd all the time. I have never had a Rolls Royce and have no desire for one.

Q: Leslie, you were recently on the David Dunseith radio program called "Talk Back." One caller phoned in to say that many years ago you had prayed for his mother and charged her £15 for the prayer.

A: I say again, no wonder over the years I refused to answer such garbage. I have prayed for tens of thousands of people personally through the laying on of hands and never once, at any time or in any place, have I ever mentioned money with regard to prayer. It is a total and absurd concoction and it is unbelievable that people can still perpetrate such falsehoods. What the man said on the David Dunseith show was a lie. I have never done such a thing and I never will.

Q: Why is it Leslie, that you take up so much time in each service talking about money?

A: It is obvious to me that whoever makes such a charge has never been in one of our services. I am a preacher of the Gospel. I seek the face of God and I study the Scriptures. In my service the vast majority of time, and I emphasize the word vast, is taken up ministering God's Word to the people. Only a very small percentage of time is taken up to receive the Lord's tithes and offerings.

I do believe strongly in giving, but as far as I know, I am not the only minister or church that receives offerings. I do not mind being criticized for what I have done, but over these many years I have been criticized for so many things that I was never guilty of. I challenge anybody to come to a number of our services to find out the percentage of time spent ministering God's Word as opposed to the time spent receiving offerings. You will find, that probably ninety-eight or ninety-nine percent of the time is spent on God's Word and only one or two percent regarding offerings.

I say it again; I believe strongly that the tithe is the Lord's, and I am not apologizing for the fact that we receive offerings. God's work needs money just like any other concern, be it a business or a family household, but people ought to get their facts right.

Q: Tell us a little more about yourself Leslie.

A: As I have already stated, I was born and raised in Belfast and I accepted Christ as a young boy. I am glad to say that through His grace I have gone on with Him in the Christian way for all these years. I love Him with every fiber of my being; and every single day I seek to serve Him and do what He asks me to do, be that in America, in Ireland, or wherever.

I can also say that God's call rings in my mind and in my spirit day and night. It's like a joke to me to hear people talk about my so-called "love of money" and other things. I need money like everybody else does to operate, but the truth is that beyond that, I don't care about the stuff. I love Jesus and I want to serve Him. In fact, my attitude has always been, and still is, based on a verse which my mother gave me as a young person; "Set your affection on things above, not on things on the earth" (Colossians 3:2).

I remember one particular man who had fought us so much. His own mother had been healed through my ministry, so he had every reason to be thankful that this ministry was even in existence. However, when he did not get his own way in our church, he turned turtle, as they say, and accused me of the very things which he was guilty of. I have never seen a man so consumed with a passion for money as that man. Evidently the press didn't care about that. They just wanted to listen to his lies about a preacher who was doing his best daily to live for God and to serve the King of Kings and the Lord of Lords.

I can say that I am totally aware that I am not a creature of time. I am a creature of eternity and I have the eternal view. That's the way I am going to live.

Q: You have said Leslie, that there were no moral failures in your life. What about mistakes?

A: Hey, hold on a minute. Let nobody imagine that there is anybody who has ever lived who didn't have mistakes except, of course, our Saviour, Jesus Christ. I have been loaded with them like everybody else. Hopefully I have learned from my mistakes, but there is a big difference between mistakes and behaviour that is either immoral or illegal. I have, however, few regrets. God has led me in a marvelous way.

As I look back, I can see that one of the main mistakes I made, especially in earlier days, was having a naive attitude and putting people into positions of authority within my ministry who simply were not fit to be there and who subsequently let the team down.

Q: Leslie, here is a different kind of question. We have mostly talked about your detractors. What about your friends?

A: Nobody will ever know how grateful I am for the way God, in His goodness and mercy, has blessed my life. He has blessed me in many ways, and I am so thankful for the wonderful family and friends He has given me all over the world.

As a matter of fact, there are pastors, evangelists, children's workers, Gospel singers, and so forth, ministering for the Lord in different countries around the world, who came to Christ in my own meetings over the years. Multitudes have been healed and filled with the Holy Spirit. I have more people than I can count. I have friends in high places and low places too, and what I am particularly grateful for are the wonderful, warm friendships that have lasted for twenty and thirty years and even more.

Several years ago, when we were going through the heat of the battle of persecution, I remember clearly one day, the Holy Spirit speaking to me in the depths of my heart. He gave me these words, which have been such a mighty blessing to me, "The people who matter are for you." I repeat, I will never forget those words. What a blessing, even to this moment. "The people who matter are for you." God has given me favour with literally thousands of people, and I feel the warmth of their love and their prayer support.

There is something else I would like to add at this point. I remember on another occasion, when the Holy Spirit spoke to me in the midst of a fierce battle. It seemed there was trouble on every side. Then these words came out of my spirit, spoken by the Holy Ghost, "If you had been more perfect" (it would seem at this point that the Lord was going to say, if you had been more perfect, then you wouldn't have been in so much trouble). I repeat, "If you had been more perfect, you would have been in more trouble; and if you had been totally perfect, they would have crucified you."

Yes, I have friends all over the world and how thankful I am for them. They are the people who matter. Of course, what can I say about my family? Maureen and I have now been married for over 46 years. It has been like one long honeymoon. Our three children are a constant blessing to us and have not given us the slightest trouble ever. They all love the Lord, and how I love them.

Q: Leslie, here is our last question. We have centered mostly on criticism. What about compliments?

A: Well you know, there's an old saying which declares, self-praise is no recommendation. So, I am certainly not going to compliment myself. I recognize I am only a lump of clay and am nothing outside of the grace of God.

I am, of course, thankful for all the expressions of gratitude which I have received from people who have been saved, healed, or filled with the Holy Spirit or blessed in some way or other through my ministry over the years. I give God the glory; but I am thankful for all those complimentary comments which number in the thousands, even in the tens of thousands.

I suppose we all like to be appreciated; and if there was any one particular thing that I would single out over the years as a compliment that touched me, then I would have to tell you about my good friend Ian Hamilton, the well-known television producer. Several years ago, Ian was making a documentary for the BBC about me and my ministry. In the course of it, he almost "lived" with us for three weeks. We literally spent hours together because he and his camera team followed us everywhere. When it was all over, Ian later told me that some of his colleagues asked him when did the mask fall off, referring to me. Ian told me that he looked at them and said, "Gentlemen, there is no mask."

As I said before, that touched me. It's true, there is no mask. I am what I am by the grace of God. I love Jesus Christ with all of my heart, and I belong to Him from the crown of my head to the soles of my feet. With His strength I will serve Him and love Him and obey Him until I see Him face to face.

NONE BUT CHRIST CAN SATISFY,

O Christ, in Thee my soul hath found,
And found in Thee alone,
The peace, the joy I sought so long,
The bliss till now unknown.

I sighed for rest and happiness,
I yearned for them, not Thee;
But, while I passed my Savior by,
His love laid hold on me.

I tried the broken cisterns, Lord,
But, ah, the waters failed;
Even as I stooped to drink they fled,
And mocked me as I wailed.

The pleasures lost I sadly mourned,
But never wept for Thee,
Till grace the sightless eyes received,
Thy loveliness to see.

Now none but Christ can satisfy,
None other Name for me!
There's love, and life, and lasting joy,
Lord Jesus, found in Thee.

Author Unknown

CHAPTER 15

I AM A HAPPY MAN

Yes, sir! I am a happy man! The only problem with that statement is that it does not come even close to describing how happy I am. So let me try again. I am a very, very, very happy man! My life is filled with peace and tranquility. I love God with every fiber of my being, and I am so grateful for **His** wonderful grace which has been so abundantly showered upon my life. It is **His** grace and **His** goodness that has produced such joy and happiness in my life.

My joy and happiness is deeply rooted in my walk with God. It is all of God's enabling, of course. I will always be grateful for my mother's prayers and the powerful work of the Holy Spirit in my life which, early on, put into me an all-consuming magnificent obsession to obey God and to follow Christ at all costs. This has resulted in over fifty years of walking talking, and obeying my fantastic Master - the Lord Jesus Christ.

Without Him I could do nothing (John 15:5). However, with Him we can do all things. It is all to God's glory. Oh how I love my Master (Exodus 21:5)!!

I fervently believe that true joy and true and lasting happiness have their foundation in honoring God and putting **Him** first in all things. We are all lumps of clay but His grace and mercy can certainly cause us to **put Him first**, thereby being blessed beyond measure.

I have never been a materialistic person. Sometimes I jokingly tell Maureen, when we are in the mall together, that I love walking around to see all the things I can get by without. However, God has a principle. It is simply that if we seek first the Kingdom of God, **all these things will be added unto us** (Matthew 6:33).

He has added **abundantly** unto me and my family, yet I only sought the **King** and not the things which were on the King's table.

I thank God for my fantastic family. Maureen and I have been married for about forty-seven years. It has been a glorious union. We married in the will of God and we continue in His blessing. Maureen is a fantastic person. She is so strong and has been an incredible help and blessing to me. If I had to do it all over again, as they say, I would do it at the drop of a hat! She is magnificent!

Maureen was greatly blessed by having a wonderful mother and a wonderful grandmother. It was these two ladies who led Maureen to Church as a child and taught her the things of God.

We have three fabulous children. Ruthanne is C.E.O. of our entire ministry. In a word, she is fantastic as she carries the whole load of this ministry. I am blessed beyond words to have her in charge with her wonderful intelligence and creativity.

Our son, Leslie, is a jet pilot captain. He flies movie-stars, celebrities, and so forth in his luxury jet. He is a terrific son and, like his two sisters, he loves the Lord with all his heart.

LaDonna Raquel is our youngest child. She is truly a wonderful, wonderful person and is in charge of our email division. LaDonna has three children, Leslie has two and Ruthanne has one.

Ruthanne and LaDonna lead the singing in our services. They are beautiful people with beautiful voices. I thank God also for our six wonderful grandchildren and also our children's spouses. Their names are Sean, Melissa, Ryan, Zoe, Kyle, Landen, Connor, and Meagan.

No wonder I am a happy, supremely contented man.

Then, there is my wonderful calling. I never asked to be a preacher and teacher of God's Word. I was an extremely shy child. I still am a basically very shy and private person. But God put this wonderful calling upon me and I am thrilled to do whatever my Father wants me to do.

Yes, I am a happy man. It is because of God's grace and the enabling He has given me throughout all these years to obey Him no matter who said what!

I could go back to any person or church or country I have visited during these approximately fifty years of ministry and say, like Paul, "**I have coveted no man's silver or gold or apparel**" (Acts 20:33).

God has enabled me to walk before Him in a clean and honorable way. I realize fully that in myself I am nothing, therefore I am thrilled to give my God all the glory for His magnificent blessings which have given me such joy, such happiness, such peace and such satisfaction in my life.

I know I have obeyed God.

I know I have followed His will relentlessly.

I know I am in His will at this very second! Praise God forever!

If I were to summarize my thoughts on true joy and lasting happiness, I would say the following:

If a person wants to experience deep peace, satisfaction, contentment, and happiness, he must know who he is and why he is here on this earth. He must be comfortable in his own skin and, at all costs, he must wear the coat that fits him. I know without the shadow of a doubt who I am. I am a servant of the most High God. I know why I am here. I have been called by God to teach His word and to explain it to the people.

My thrill is not in the preaching or teaching but in obeying Jesus all these years.

If that includes preaching and teaching, that is fine but the joy is in the obedience. Other than obeying God, I have utterly no desire to ever be in the pulpit nor in front of a TV camera.

All of this makes me comfortable in my own skin. I am wearing the coat that fits me. I know I can help people. I know I can teach them God's Word if they will stand still long enough to listen.

As the Psalmist says in Psalm 87:7, "All my springs are in thee."

I, too, can say that. All my peace and satisfaction is in thee, oh Lord!!

In closing, I want to give thanks to God also for the many, many wonderful friends I have made over the years. They are too numerous to count and they are scattered over several countries. As I say, I thank God for every one of them. I will mention at this point only two. They are Kurt and Roland, the

Swedish singers and guitarists. Our deep fellowship started over forty years ago and we have held meetings together in various countries.

On one occasion when we were holding a crusade in downtown Belfast something amazing happened. One night, as I was preaching—in the middle of the sermon—a number of people got up and started moving down the aisles toward me. I was completely taken by surprise.

For a moment I did not realize what was happening. Suddenly it came to me. They were coming to be saved. The conviction of the Holy Spirit was so strong that they could wait no longer. There were many others instances of wonderful demonstrations of God's power. One man observed, "It was revival." He was right. The meetings were so anointed and glorious. I will always thank God for my friendship with Kurt and Roland. True friends indeed.

AMAZING GRACE

Amazing grace! How sweet the sound
That saved a wretch like me!
I once was lost, but now am found;
Was blind, but now I see.

'Twas grace that taught my heart to fear,
And grace my fears relieved;
How precious did that grace appear
The hour I first believed!

Through many dangers, toils and snares,
I have already come;
'Twas grace hath brought me safe thus far,
And grace will lead me home.

The Lord has promised good to me,
His Word my hope secures;
He will my Shield and Portion be,
As long as life endures.

When we've been there ten thousand years,
Bright shining as the sun,
We've no less days to sing God's praise
Than when we'd first begun.

John Newton

CHAPTER 16

TESTIMONIALS

Over the years we have received literally thousands of wonderful, inspiring messages.

Here are five: two from America, two from Ireland, and one from our local congregation in Tarpon Springs, Florida.

Over thirty years ago, when I was a young man of about twenty, I visited Mount Paran Church in Atlanta. There was a guest speaker that day and his delightful Irish accent, which struck me as a pleasant curiosity, increased my interest. Since the church was quite large, I could not distinguish his face.

After this Irishman, Leslie Hale, began his remarks, almost immediately I began to pay attention in earnest. It wasn't just that the speaker was unusually skillful, which he certainly was; but I felt something more substantial drawing me into the message. Today, I know that was the Holy Spirit. This man had something to say, and his message was important. What I couldn't know then was that the outcome of my life would depend upon hearing it.

Leslie spoke on the myth of the Christmas message as it is taught today. You know the one: three wise men follow a bright star unerringly to the manger and present the newborn Christ-child with gifts. Only, as Leslie pointed out, that story isn't in the Bible. The Bible records that a group of men from the east, men of influence and wealth inspired by a star, set out on a journey to worship a new born king. But the star goes out, they become lost, and they look and feel like fools. To make matters worse, they go to King Herod for help and discern that he intends to kill the child; literally, to kill their dream! Lost, out of options, and confused, they had to ask, "Did we really hear from God?

Are we fools? If God wanted us to do this, what happened to the star? Why have we been abandoned?" Leslie titled his message, "What to Do When You Lose Your Way."

Have you ever wanted to really do something with your life, to have a life beyond the ordinary? I did. Leslie was teaching any future achievers in that audience one of the most important principles in the Bible: Once you begin to pursue your dream, that bright star of high hopes will go dark for a season. During those trials you will have to decide whether to believe that God is there when you can't hear or feel Him or return home beaten.

The star reappeared for the Magi, and they "rejoiced with exceeding joy." They met the Christ-child as a young boy of about two in his parent's home and worshipped Him. Their dream was fulfilled. The Bible later records that, "They which sought the young child's life are dead." Leslie's message was that this is an allegory for every Christian life. If you will trust God, even when your star goes out, He will not lead you to the death of your dream but to the realization of it. Our God, Leslie said, is the God of every detour and every detail. That was being affirmed in my own life; it was not chance that had me visit that day. Many years later, that message would sustain me through some very dark times.

I bought a recording of Leslie's message on the way out. (I remember debating it. Four dollars was an expense worth weighing at the time.) I put the tape away and went about my young life. I never heard the name of Leslie Hale mentioned again. Years later, I became a police officer in Marietta, Georgia; but the desire to achieve burned too brightly for me to stay in that line of work. Some people wish to excel in music or sports; for me it was business. I wanted to work for myself. I wanted to be financially free. I left the police department to pursue that dream – and what I went through for the next sixteen years I would not wish on an enemy.

One difficult day I happened across an old cassette tape in a remote drawer: "What to Do When You Lose Your Way." I put it in my truck and listened to it and kept listening to it for the next fifteen years. Every time I thought that I could not go on, I would pull out that tape and listen to some man in thick Irish brogue tell me to keep going; assuring me that even when my star goes out, it is part of God's plan to bring me to my dream. I literally drew life out of that tape.

Well, I finally won out and I can tell you from the heart that I did not do it on talent. I think life finally said, "The fool does not know when he is beat! Pay him off so that we can move on." "The fool" had a Leslie Hale tape in his back pocket! I am certain that my brief contact with this man was orchestrated by God, proving Leslie's point from thirty years ago – Our God is the God of the detail, and if you will trust Him and persist, he can and will bring you through to the realization of your dream! Hallelujah!

A few years ago I was walking through my den and the television was on. I heard a voice that I knew instantly. It was that Irish preacher who was on my twenty-five year old cassette tape! I ran to the television screen, anxious to get my first look at the face of Leslie Hale. I noted that he had a ministry in Tampa, Florida. I sent a letter letting him know that I would be supporting his work. I began to receive a copy of his weekly teachings. My wife and I were overwhelmed by what we heard. I told my wife, "We can't learn these things anywhere else. Why aren't other ministers teaching this? These biblical truths are amazing!" A few months later my office manager said, "There's a Leslie Hale on the phone for you." I couldn't have been more surprised if she had announced the president in person.

One of the disappointing things about getting older and wiser is that you begin to see the world as it is. Ben Franklin wrote, "Those that understand the world best like it the least." Unfortunately, that sobering assessment can occasionally apply to Christian ministries. I know. There is a lot of money and public acclaim involved, and it takes an exceptional man or woman not to be influenced by it. The choreographed appeals can bring in fortunes. For some in public ministries, those factors do become motivations rather than means to service. That is not an indictment of ministry work. It is just an observation of human frailty.

I am honored to tell you that I have become friends with Leslie Hale over these last few years. Our relationship is deep, spontaneous, effortless, and obviously refreshing to us both. Leslie Hale Ministries uses no tricks, no schemes - ever. Why? What is different here? Though he is involved with projects of great expense and importance, no appeals so common today such as "send money for your financial breakthrough" is offered. No; God's rich blessings, Leslie teaches, come without price – save the blood of Christ. He teaches the total sufficiency of the living Christ and he lives it in his ministry. You should support his work if you are fed by it; but you will hear no gimmicks. Christ alone is his supply.

Leslie holds Christ up as a jeweler would raise a diamond to light, explaining the inter-working of the facets to raise your admiration for the beauty. Like a miner laboring in the depths of the earth to bring forth precious hidden things, Leslie mines God's Word for its deep truths and brings them out to share with all who will listen and learn. Leslie is a teacher. He teaches men and women to live victoriously through the power of God's Word. I am anxious to read this remarkable man's life story.

MARK ASHE, GEORGIA USA

It has been my privilege to know Leslie Hale, as a friend and brother, for over 35 years. I have had a sincere appreciation for his balanced and fruitful ministry. Leslie has always been faithful to the consensus of Scripture and never embraced an isolated view, even if it was popular to do so at the time. His integrity and honesty always stand out in all his relationships with other people. He is a family man and lives his life according to God's moral and ethical standards. I am glad to be associated with Leslie Hale.

CORDIALLY, PASTOR DAN BELLER, D. MIN.
OKLAHOMA USA

I have known Leslie Hale for more than 34 years now. He is a dynamic preacher and the most anointed servant of God I have ever known. Leslie's ministry has been a great blessing to many thousands of people and many have been saved, healed, and delivered through it.

I have never known anyone who is so enthusiastic, positive, and does his best to serve God and help people than Leslie Hale. He is God's man, and it has been my privilege to know him and sit under his ministry these many years. His kindness and goodness are beyond words.

I was saved in Leslie's meetings on the January 14, 1973. I thank God for a totally honest man, preaching a totally honest message.

Albert Tufts (Jnr.) Belfast, Northern Ireland

I have known Pastor Leslie Hale since November 1975, when my wife, Lorraine and I accepted Jesus Christ as our personal Saviour at Faith Tabernacle in York Road, Belfast. Since then, I have come to appreciate Leslie Hale as a wonderful preacher and teacher of God's Word, indeed the best that I have ever heard, and I have heard many.

In recent years many preachers, who at one time were good men of God, have gone astray in various ways. However, I am pleased to say that I am part of the Leslie Hale Ministry, where the senior Pastor Leslie has stayed true to the principles of the Bible which never change.

Leslie is obviously a man who is in touch with God and is greatly anointed by the Holy Spirit. We are a happy family with a real meaning to our lives. God gets the glory but we thank God for Leslie Hale.

Isaac Doyle, Belfast, Northern Ireland.

What God's Word means to me.

I owe my eternal life to God through Jesus Christ. I owe my day to day life to Leslie Hale. That is not an exaggeration!!

There is a lot to be said for individual Bible reading and study. However, there is more to be said for someone who can open the Word of God and teach it. Leslie Hale is a man who hears from Heaven, regularly, and can open the Word of God like a flower in all its beauty and splendor. When it comes to learning of God and His ways, there are no such terms as "fast food" or "drive through." It takes time, effort, and the Holy Spirit's help to become a disciplined learner, a disciple. It also takes someone who is truly committed to God and to ministering His Word. The teacher who will, without ceasing, consistently present only what God says and not his own opinions, who creates within the student an insatiable desire for God, and who will, with tremendous care and respect for God's Word, present the Gospel as just that: the Good News!

When I think of all that I have learned and am learning about God and the person of His Son, Jesus Christ, I know that I learned it all here, sitting under the teaching of one of the greatest Bible teachers of the twentieth century, bar none!

J.B.
MEMBER OF LESLIE'S LOCAL CONGREGATION,
TARPON SPRINGS, FLORIDA

POETRY

I love poetry. When I was very young, both at school and at work, my mother was always home when I got home. I only remember one time when I got home and the house was empty. In turn I had to go out before they could return, so I first left them a little note which said,

> "He went to work,
> They went for a run,
> He fed himself like the prodigal son,
> Juvenile delinquents, need we ask why?
> When parents leave home without saying good-bye!"

I make no claim to be a poet and yet several years ago, I wrote a number of little pieces. Of recent years, I seem to be so preoccupied with God's call upon my life that I have written none at all.

I would like to share with you some of my poems, just as I wrote them several years ago as a young man.

JESUS IS CONTEMPORARY

Jesus is contemporary - as tomorrow morning's sun,
As tomorrow morning's news-flash - as a new life just begun,
He's up-to-date and modern and real exciting too,
He's fresh and keen and lively, as the early morning dew.

A hundred million years and more, in existence He has been.
But today He's still involved in our youthful, modern scene.
Jet planes and radar and television too Are old compared to
Jesus Christ - for He is ever new.

Jesus knows my every need, my every longing too,
For Jesus lives within my heart - and not beyond the blue.
And if you'll take Him in today - you never will be sorry
For Jesus Christ is not old fashioned - He is contemporary!

It's not so much the place we work or how we wear our clothes,
The thing that counts with God above is where our worship goes.
For fashions change and men would try to tell us what to do
But God deals with the inner man - and creates it all anew!

MY KINSMAN-REDEEMER

Why should I keep on struggling, why have a tempest within,
Why should I keep on fighting, o'er the problem of sin?
On the cross He suffered, paid the full debt for me
Stood in my place, saved me by grace, my Kinsman-Redeemer is He!

My Kinsman-Redeemer has come - my sins have been washed away,
My fears and frustration are gone - I'll walk with Him each day,
The Divine substitute is He - Oh wondrous plan of love,
I'm accepted as a son - by the one who reigns above!

I'm now "accepted in the beloved" - not by works of my own,
I throw my weight upon - He who sits on the throne,
My greatest works could not atone for any misdemeanour,
I'm saved because of Jesus Christ - my own Kinsman-Redeemer!

Here is one I wrote on Psalm 48. As I read this Psalm, the 14 verses seemed to fall into eight categories:

1. The song of Zion (verse 1)
2. The situation of Zion (verse 2)
3. The secret of Zion (verse 3)
4. The sacrilege of Zion (verse 4 - 7)
5. The sight of Zion (verse 8)
6. The servants of Zion (verses 9 - 11)
7. The strength of Zion (verses 12 - 13)

8. The security of Zion (verse 14)
Under these headings I wrote the following poem:

ZION, CITY OF OUR GOD

Zion has a noble SONG and nobler still its theme,
T'was not thought up by mortal man -
it was our Father's dream,
The SONG of Zion - and its theme,
its beginning and its end
Is centered in the Christ Himself
our Savior and our friend.

The SITUATION of the church
is lovely to behold,
The place where it is built upon
shall not at all grow old,
The Saviour's shoulders bear it up,
His arms around it go,
But this our song - we rest upon
His precious crimson flow.

The SECRET of the church is this,
our God is with us still,
His power is in our palaces,
we joy to do His will,
A refuge strong He'll always be,
for those who're in distress
And all who come to Him can shout,
"I have been truly blessed."

The SACRILEGE of Zion
is a burden on our hearts,
It always hurts our spirits
when we see it torn in parts,
But a resurrection wind
is blowing from the East
To smash old Satan's Tarshish ships
and prepare us for the feast.

As we have heard so we have SEEN
the Psalmist did declare,
God hath fulfilled His promises
each one with loving care,
For He who spake doth also act
to bring each into being
So rest assured, if you have heard,
you'll soon be also seeing!

His SERVANTS all, we think of Him,
as we journey on our way,
We'll praise Him all around the world
until our closing day,
And then He'll take Mount Zion home,
for the marriage of the Lamb,
And there we'll join the heavenly choir,
in our eternal psalm!

Walk around old Zion's wall,
it's solid and secure,
The towers and palaces are STRONG,
the bulwarks will endure,
We'll tell the story of its power
to all who follow after,
For Zion's bondage hath been smashed
our mouths are filled with laughter!

This God is ours - He'll always be
right unto our death,
And even after that He'll be
our every living breath,
For when this earthly life is o'er
and we lie beneath the sod,
We'll be SECURE on Zion's Mount
The city of our God!

It is so good to see someone make up his mind to achieve a goal and then go out and accomplish it. Here is one along that theme.

SEE IT THROUGH

Be firm and sure as you travel along,
And soon you'll sing the victor's song,
And join in the triumphant throng,
SEE IT THROUGH!

Keep praising God through day and night,
The victor's crown is in your sight
And soon you will attain the height,
SEE IT THROUGH!

Keep going on when all seems black,
For He will give you all you lack,
Whate'er you do - don't turn back,
SEE IT THROUGH!

The clouds are parting - the sun comes through,
Look up - your skies are turning blue,
And now there's one more thing to do
SEE IT THROUGH!

And when you clasp the victor's cup
And you and the Master sit down and sup,
You'll be so glad you didn't give up
SEE IT THROUGH!

So though the storm is all around,
Give praise to God - it's the victory sound,
And the prize by you will soon be found
SEE IT THROUGH!

The fight is over and you've come through,
For a time it seemed impossible to do
What you have done will help others too,
YOU'VE SEEN IT THROUGH!!

This one is centered around the Bible story found in Luke 5.

JESUS MAKES THE DIFFERENCE

They gathered in from here and there
to catch Him in His word,
"The Man's a fake," they cried,
"His teachings are absurd."
But Jesus had this ace
His presence you could feel
And faith and power were evident
for God was there to heal!

A man was carried down the street,
His name I do not know.
Just another case was he
with sickness he was low,
But faithful friends then ripped the roof
and gently let him down
And Jesus cast His eyes toward the man
upon the ground.

Jesus saw the outline of the man's
face struck with pain,
And quickly opened up His love
and forgiveness made plain
No longer was this precious man
a sinner in the crowd,
He had met Jesus "face to face"
and he was mighty proud!

The grace of God was then out-poured
"Your sins are all forgiven,"
The sinful man had been redeemed
He now was bound for heaven,
Transformed by Jesus' power right there
his load of sin was gone.
The guilty feeling was removed
and in his heart a song!

But satan ever lurks around
to criticize and blame,
"How can this man forgive his sins
and hence remove his shame?"
The Pharisees and Scribes did
in their hearts complain,
"We are the 'super race,'" they thought,
and clearly showed disdain.

But Jesus set the pace that day,
their answer He did give,
"Which is the easiest to do?
To heal or to forgive?
For all is easy unto me
Divinity I prove,
By blessing you and others too
and troubled minds I soothe!"

Then turning to the man again,
He quickly made this cry,
"Take up your bed and walk today
you shall no longer lie."
The man did brace himself just then
and jumped up to his feet,
He was so different from the one
they carried down the street!

Everybody present there
could scarce believe their eyes,
For Jesus had exposed the Scribes
and their outrageous lies,
He had indeed proved He was God
He had Salvation's plan,
With not a trace of Satan left
in or on the man!

The place was changed right there and then
amazed were all the crowd,
At what the Nazarene could do
they spoke His praise aloud,
And any place on earth is changed
when Jesus has His way
And men declare, when He is there
We've seen strange things today!"

How can I sum up for you now
this story so exciting?
I'll tell you one more truth I've learned
to help you keep on fighting.
When Satan comes to worry you
remember he has lost
And all Salvation's plan is yours
and Jesus pays the cost!

Leslie can be seen live at www.LeslieHale.com each Sunday (10 a.m. EST) and each Wednesday (7:30 p.m. EST). His telecast is also seen weekly throughout the United States, Canada, and overseas.

istry Headquarters including Bible College, Dining Room, and Sanctuary

The beautiful lobby

Beautiful dining faciliticies in use each week serving great food ar
providing warm fellowship. The food is always complimentary.

The Antique Bible Museum housing one of the finest private collections of Bibles in the world.

Artist's Impression of the life-size "Tabernacle In The Wilderness"
(Now nearing completion in a purpose-built facility on the south
side of our headquarters).

Who will ever forget those fantastic meetings in the Ulster Hall,
Belfast at the height of "The Troubles."

My father was the greatest
accordionist I ever heard.

My parents were wonderful.
They were married for 52 years.

A marriage made in Heaven.
Relaxing at home in Tarpon Springs, Florida with wife, Maureen.

Leslie's sisters, Doreen and Ella, from Belfast.

Leslie Hale, Wife Maureen, and family

First church and headquarters building,
York Road, Belfast, Northern Ireland

'Revival' with Leslie (center) with Kurt and Roland, singers
and musicians from Sweden